P9-DXH-583

DAUGHTERS OF THE GODDESS

DAUGHTERS OF THE GODDESS

The Women Saints of India

Linda Johnsen

Yes International Publishers
St. Paul, Minnesota

Riverside Community College
Library
SEP   '96   4800 Magnolia Avenue
Riverside, California 92506

BL 1241.44 .L56 1994

Johnsen, Linda, 1954-

Daughters of the goddess

cation Data

Linda, Johnsen, 1954-
    Daughters of the goddess: the women saints of India / Linda
Johnsen. — 1st Yes International pbk. ed.
        p.   cm.
    Includes bibliographical references.
    ISBM 0-936663-09-X : $12.95
    1. Women saints—India. 2. Hindu saints—India.   I. Title.
BL 1241.44.L56   1994
294.5'092'2—dc20
[B]   93-46194
                                                        CIP

Copyright © 1994 by Linda Johnsen. All rights reserved. No part of this book
may be used or reproduced in any manner whatsoever without written
permission except in the case of brief quotations embodied in critical articles
and reviews. For information and permissions address:
        Yes International Publishers
        1317 Summit Avenue
        St. Paul, Minnesota 55105-2602
        612-645-6808.

Printed in the United States of America.

FIRST YES INTERNATIONAL PAPERBACK EDITION PUBLISHED IN 1994.

Cover Photo: Sri Ma of Kamakhya

Contents

Acknowledgments   vii

Daughters of the Goddess   1

Contemporary Hindu Women Saints   21

Sri Ma of Kamakhya: Living the Goddess   29

Anandamayi Ma: The Bliss Permeated Mother   47

Anandi Ma: Mastering the Kundalini   58

Gurumayi Chidvilasananda: Beauty and Grace   73

Ma Yoga Shakti: No Nonsense Yogini   86

Ammachi: In the Lap of the Mother   95

Incarnating the Feminine Divine   111

Resources   122

Further Reading   123

Glossary   125

Acknowledgments

Portions of this book originally appeared in *Yoga Journal* and *Yoga International*. I'd like to express my appreciation to the staff of both these magazines for consistently bringing the stories of India's women of spirit to the attention of the American public.

Thank you Johnathan, for deflecting my half of the rent while this book was being written! (Janardanananda, as Sri Ma affectionately calls my husband, is a true *putro devyah,* son of the Mother Divine. I don't think even Sita had a better partner. Jai Janardan!)

Pranams to Pandit Rajmani Tigunait, who first led this uncouth, overly heady agnostic into the temple of Sri Vidya and introduced me to the Goddess.

I also want to thank the Goddess at the Brahma Yoni Mandir outside Gaya. When, devastated by cholera, I was weeping with frustration at being too weak to climb the hundreds of stairs to worship at her shrine, she came down the mountain and entered my mind in the form of hours of ecstatic meditation. When I finally rose, my strength had been restored. Without her grace, I could not have completed this pilgrimage.

Om Aim Sarasvatyai Namaha!
Om Shrim Lakshmyai Namaha!
Om Hrim Kali Durge Namaha!
Om Amriteshvaryai Namaha!

DAUGHTERS
OF THE
GODDESS

"*I*ndia has produced more saints per capita than any other culture in history, it seems," I mention to the pandit between bites of *chapati*. "There are hundreds of them, from Buddha to Mahatma Gandhi, Ramakrishna, Ramana Maharshi, Paramahansa Yogananda. Why aren't there any Indian women saints?"

Pandit Rajmani looks up in surprise. We are having dinner Indian style, seated crosslegged around a white tablecloth neatly spread over the living room floor. "There are thousands of lady saints in India. You think because there are no books about them, they do not exist."

The pandit's wife is watching us from the kitchen door, ready to descend with ladles full of curry should any empty space appear on our thin, stainless steel plates. Following Indian custom, she will not eat until her guests are finished. I want to respect the norms of her culture, but frankly this makes me extremely uncomfortable.

"If you go into the Himalayas you will find many *bhairavis*, female yogis who live in the caves and forests doing penance. But most of the women saints remain with their families, purifying themselves by serving others. Every morning before their family awakens they sit before the altars in their homes, worshiping and praying. They don't care for name and fame. Even the people in the next village do not know who they are. In your country you believe that no one can be a saint unless they give seminars."

I have not touched my yogurt; I can't figure out how to eat it with my fingers. I watch Rajmani stir a handful of fragrant basmati rice into his yogurt, and pop the dripping ball of grain into his mouth.

"You have heard of Agastya?" he continues. I nod, recognizing the name of the legendary Vedic *brahmarishi* (God-realized seer). "He was a great sage, one of the greatest that has lived. And yet he felt that his realization was incomplete. He wanted to be initiated in Sri Vidya, the supreme secret knowledge of the Goddess. He had heard that there was a master of this tradition in a province far away, and one day he set out to find him. In those days travelling was done by foot, so it took many months to reach this man. But when he reached there the master told him, 'Sorry, I cannot initiate you. Actually, you are already more advanced than I am. The only one qualified to teach you is my own guru, the founder of this lineage.'

"Agastya became very excited. 'Where can I find this great guru?' he asked. The master told him the name of the province where his guru lived. Agastya was shocked. 'But that's *my* province!' he said. It made him ashamed to learn that such a great teacher was living nearby and he had never noticed. He had thousands of students himself; it never occurred to him that a teacher greater than himself might live in the same region.

"Then the master told him the name of the village where his guru lived. 'But that's *my* village!' Agastya said. He was even more embarrassed. And then the master described the house where his guru lived. 'But that's *my* house!' Agastya said. Agastya was a short man, but now he felt two inches tall. Finally the master told him the name of his guru, the fully realized, supreme master Lopamudra. 'But that's my *wife!*' Agastya cried." Rajmani laughs and winks at Mira, still standing in the doorway with her pot of curry. Her eyes twinkle.

This tale sheds light on one of my favorite accounts from the ancient Hindu scriptures called the Vedas. "Sir, do you remember the story where Agastya is busy with his ascetic practices and Lopamudra sidles up to him and asks him to make love to her? At first he resists, but she's very persistent, and finally he gives in. I thought the text would end by saying, 'And then Agastya lost the fruit of a thousand years of rigorous penance,' like many of the yogic scriptures say whenever anyone slips up and has sex. But the text ends, 'Agastya became an even mightier sage, for he nourished both the paths of renunciation and of secular life.'"

"Yes, yes! At first Agastya believed that self mortification was the only way to realize God. Lopamudra showed him that worldly life, when it is imbued with divine awareness, can also lead one to God. It was not a seduction, but an initiation. Lopamudra was a master of Sri Vidya. She knew the Goddess. She understood the Tantra."

"But women like her were rare."

Rajmani smiles at me. "Not at all. You know that in the Hindu religion, we say that all beings are divine. At heart we are all one with God."

"Yes, Panditji. That's one of the things that attracted me to India."

"But did you know that the first person to declare this unity was a woman? There is a passage called the Devi Sukta in our most ancient scripture, the *Rig Veda*. Realizing that she was one with the Cosmic Mother, the seer Ambhrini sang—" and Rajmani begins to chant in Vedic. I cannot follow the archaic Sanskrit but I remember the hymn, one of the most famous in the Vedas.

> I am the Queen, source of thought, knowledge itself!
> You do not know me, yet you dwell in me.
> I announce myself in words both gods
> and humans welcome.
> From the summit of the world, I give birth to the sky!
> The tempest is my breath, all living creatures are my life!
> Beyond the wide earth, beyond the vast heaven,
> My grandeur extends forever!

In the rapture of her meditation, Ambhrini had discovered the Mother of the Universe at the core of her own being.

The pandit's wife serves us *gulab jamen,* fried dough balls soaked in sugar syrup. I take the opportunity to ask her, "Mira, did you hear about women saints when you were growing up?"

"When I was a girl my heroine was Mira Bai. I was named after her. She had many problems in her life because she was more devoted to God than to her husband, but today there is no village in India where her songs are not sung."

"India's women saints are the crown jewels in her tiara. They are the daughters of the Goddess," Rajmani says. "You should learn more about them. There are many great women saints in

India even today." Rajmani, who has been tutoring me in Sanskrit, knows I like to write. "Perhaps you should do a book."

I laugh at his suggestion, but resolve to discover more about India's "crown jewels."

§

Rajastan. The 16th century. Mira Bai was five years old. There was a commotion in the street; she raced to the window to see what was going on.

"It's a wedding procession," Mira's mother explained. "That gentleman there is the groom. He is on his way to meet his bride."

"Who is *my* husband?" Mira demanded.

"Lord Krishna is your husband," her mother answered, pointing to the image of the family deity on their household altar, the cowherd prince Krishna. Holding a flute to his sensuous lips, the deity smiled at them both.

A serious problem with far-reaching consequences quickly developed. Mira did not understand that her mother was joking. At first it was amusing to watch the small child bringing dishes of hot food to offer to the statue, to listen to her clanging her cymbols as she sang before the image, first the devotional songs her parents had taught her, and then charming tunes she composed herself. But as the years passed and Mira continued to sit before Krishna, earnestly singing of her love, her parents began to fear for her sanity. It was time to find her a real husband.

In this they were spectacularly successful. Bhojraj, prince of Chittor, was passing through town when he overheard a lovely voice singing passionately of God. His ear led him to Mira, whose radiance stopped the breath in his throat. A marriage proposal was quickly delivered to her parents. They were thrilled.

Mira, however, was shattered. But there was no getting out of it: her parents, who simply did not understand that she was already married, forced Mira to go through with the ceremony, and at the court of Chittor in northwest India Mira went through the motions of dutiful Hindu wifehood. As soon as her daily responsibilities were over, however, she would flee to her private meditation chamber to offer her devotions to Krishna.

Prince Bhojraj quickly discovered that being attracted to a God-intoxicated mystic was one thing; having to live with one was another. Mira's singleminded devotion soon got on his nerves, and the rest of his relatives were convinced that Mira was a lunatic. Their religion taught them that wholehearted surrender to God was the highest ideal, but consummate politicians like the Chittor royal family understood that such ideals are useful for manipulating the simpleminded; they are not to be taken literally. Mira was forbidden to worship God within the palace precincts.

Now something truly shocking happened. Mira picked up her image of Krishna and went to the public temple to worship. Waves of fury reverberated through the palace. It was unthinkable for a high caste woman to worship in a town temple with the common people. But as Mira's popularity with the local inhabitants soared, crowds of them gathering each time she appeared to listen to her songs and join in her ecstatic dance, her popularity at home floundered desperately. Several attempts were made on Mira's life, orchestrated by her exasperated mother-in-law.

These failed assassinations are the stuff of legends. The poison turned to nectar as it met Mira's lips. The adder became a garland as she placed it around her neck. The thick nails laid in her bed felt to her like lotus petals; while Mira's thwarted relatives fumed, she slept soundly. Today one wonders if these stories are not metaphorical, but suffice to say that for four centuries Indians have understood these episodes literally.

News of Mira's extraordinary devotion spread through the nearby provinces drawing hundreds, and then thousands, of devotees who came to worship with her. Word finally reached Akbar, the Muslim emperor of India, and disguised as a Hindu monk, he came to see the princess saint himself. Learning later that this bitter enemy had touched the feet of his wife, Bhojraj could bear no more. Mira was exiled.

Surrounded by devotees, Mira cheerfully began a pilgrimage to the holy sites associated with the life of the divine incarnation Krishna: Vrindaban, where he grew up, tending cows and flirting with the milkmaids; Mathura, where he overthrew the rapacious king Kamsa; Dwaraka, where he ruled till his death in 3,102 B.C.E. At home, events took a less felicitous turn. The country was stricken by draught, and the common folk were convinced it was Bhojraj's fault. Obviously Krishna was punishing the king for the pernicious way he treated Mira. Chastened, Bhojraj made a pilgrimage of his own, seeking out his wife to beg her return for the sake of his starving people.

Mira went back and was awarded full religous freedom as long as her husband remained alive. Unfortunately, after his death Mira's in-laws renewed their attacks and Mira left once again, this time for good. She wandered freely throughout northern India, beside herself with love for God, spontaneously composing songs like these:

Let me see You Lord, for without You I can't live!
Without You I'm a lotus without a pond, a moonless
      night.
I long for You every moment, roaming like a
      madwoman
Gasping in agony at my separation from You!
Days pass without food, nights without sleep:
The pain is more than I can express!

Where can I go? I can only wait for Thee.
Why are You delaying, You who dwell in the heart of
      all beings?
Master, grant me Your grace for I am Your servant
For all my lives to come.
Lord, I faint with love and yearning
At Your sacred, lotus-like feet!

People were convinced Mira was the reincarnation of Radha, the village girl who pursued Krishna throughout Vrindavan and became his favorite lover. Krishna left for Mathura to fulfill his political destiny, and Radha pined for him every moment for the rest of her life. In the evocative religious iconography of Hinduism, Radha, and thus Mira, embodied the human soul as it passionately seeks the divine.

According to legend, at a very advanced age, while dancing in ecstacy, Mira fell onto her idol of Krishna. The brass statue reached out to catch her and her body vanished, without a trace, into the smiling image. Perhaps what the biographers who chronicled this event meant to say was that in the final moments of her life the last vestige of Mira's selfhood was annihilated in divine being. At any rate, her death is said to have occurred at Dwaraka in 1550, and to this day devotees travel thousands of miles to sing and pray at the spot where God received Mira's final offering.

Mira Bai is probably the best loved of India's women saints, but there are numerous others. Akka Mahadevi, a devotee of the God Shiva, was even more flagrant than Mira in flaunting social conventions. Mahadevi was part of the Vira Shaivite ("Heroes of Shiva") movement which caused an uproar in South India in the twelfth century A.D. The Vira Shaivites were social renegades who rejected caste distinctions, sexism, and ritualism, creating a small egalitarian counterculture in which burning love for God informed their work and relationships.

Mahadevi, like Mira, was the subject of unwanted attention from a local chieftan. When Kaushika, a Kannadan prince, threatened to kill her parents if she did not consent to marriage, Mahadevi agreed to marry him on three conditions: he must never come between her and her fellow devotees, between her and her guru, or between her and Shiva. Kaushika gleefully accepted the terms.

One day not long after the wedding, Mahadevi was sleeping when a group of devotees came by to visit. Not wishing to disturb his wife, the chieftan sent them away. When Mahadevi discovered what had happened, she let him know he was down for one. On another occasion Kaushika caught her arm to prevent her from rushing out to welcome her guru, who had just arrived, because she was not yet completely dressed. He was down for two. Finally, overcome with how beautiful his wife looked as she sat in meditation, the chieftan sat down behind her and embraced her. His touch disturbed her one-pointed concentration on Lord Shiva. Kaushika was down for the count, having broken all three conditions of their marital contract by Mahadevi's somewhat rigorous interpretation. She was out the door.

Kaushika was determined to get Mahadevi back. Converting to Shaivism, he appealed to the Shaivite community to convince his wife to return. Now that the chieftan had become a worshiper of Shiva, this seemed reasonable to the devotees, and a delegation was sent to speak with Mahadevi. They found her in the mountains, naked, completely absorbed in meditation. Impressed by the *shakti* (spiritual power) emanating from her, the messengers went back to inform Kaushika that it was not their place to disturb this yogini, nor his place either.

It was not long after this that Mahadevi made her way to Kalyana and met the founders of Vira Shaivism: the great saints and social reformers Basavanna and Allama. Their sect was considered radical for that historical epoch, but Mahadevi was radical even by their standards, and she was closely cross-examined before being admitted into the heart of the community. Although nude male *sadhus* (wandering ascetics) had long been a feature of the Indian landscape (in fact, some portions of the large Jain population typically went about "clad only in the sky"), it was a shock to see a woman walking the streets without any clothes. Asked why she refused to wear a sari, Mahadevi explained that she no longer took orders from men. She had renounced the world completely; her only possession was her love for God. Since the sight of her body was so unsettling to many of those present, she let her black hair fall down freely, covering her genitals, so that they would not be disturbed.

Though Mahadevi's admission into the Vira Shaivite community was rocky, it was quickly acknowledged that she was perhaps the greatest devotee of them all. She did not hold back anything in her surrender to God. The intensity of her commitment awed the South Indians of her time, and she became a living legend.

Some of Mahadevi's sayings have crossed the centuries; thus she still speaks to us today. She compared the human soul to a silkworm spinning a smothering cocoon out of its own greed, and asked Shiva, "my beautiful Lord, white as jasmine" to cut us free. She compared *maya,* the force of illusion and desire that keeps souls pinned to the wheel of transmigration and planets spinning in their tiresome orbits, to a cowherd, herding the worlds with stick held high. Describing the totality of her surrender to God, she said, "If I am caught in the monsoon rain, I accept the waters as my bath. If I am caught in an avalanche, I take the falling rocks as flowers for my hair. If my head falls from my shoulders, my beautiful Lord Shiva, accept it as my offering to you!"

Mahadevi next left for Srishaila, a mountain sacred to Shiva, to consummate her mystical union with God. The last of her famous verses suggest that she found him there, losing herself in an all pervading reality beyond form and thought. "I cannot describe what this is. I cannot say that it is union or harmony. Having merged in my Lord, white as jasmine, I have nothing more to say whatsoever." She died in her early twenties.

Back in Kalyana, the Vira Shaivites shocked all Kannada when they celebrated the marriage of a high caste bride to a low caste groom. The king determined to protect the caste system and restore order: he sent in the militia. The Vira Shaivites were massacred. Perhaps it is just as well Mahadevi sought a higher reality in the mountains.

Bad marriages frequently spurred Indian women to immerse themselves in spiritual life. In fourteenth century Kashmir, an indifferent husband and a vicious mother-in-law drove Lalleshvari to God. Lalla patiently struggled for twelve years to make her marriage work before she finally realized that continuing to play the role of the ideal, submissive wife in the face of continual abuse was not noble; it was stupid. She fled to the home of her guru, Sri Siddhanath, where she learned and practiced the essence of Tantra: Kashmir Shaivism.

Tantra is a tradition of spiritual practice that has flourished in India since before the beginning of recorded history. Brahminism, on the other hand, is the religion of the orthodox upper caste Hindu which outwardly emphasizes lengthy and exacting rituals, and inwardly secret knowledge of higher states of awareness passed from father to son. Tantra, however, is the religion of the masses, of those who long to experience the divine presence in their hearts despite the fact that their caste or gender technically bars them from this knowledge.

To qualify for the teachings of the Vedas in a traditional brahmin household, one must be the son of a brahmin or the male, upper caste student of one. This was not always so. The Vedas themselves speak of a time when the Gayatri mantra and other sacred Hindu teachings were also passed on to women. Numerous great women scholars and mystics are mentioned in the Vedas; in fact, portions of the Vedas themselves were composed by women. Unfortunately, apparently even before the time of Buddha (circa 500 B.C.E.), women's status in Indian society began to decline and holy teachings were generally reserved for an upper class male elite.

Side by side with this orthodox system, Tantra flourished underground. Unlike Brahminism, to qualify for the teachings of Tantra one had only to be sincere, self disciplined, and motivated. There were no social bars. Over the millennia, Tantra was practiced quietly in order to avoid exciting the fundamentalists who found caste mixing offensive. The admission of women to tantric proceedings led to charges that Tantra was a "yoga of sex," a claim that was probably about as accurate as the Roman belief that early Christians who took "the body and blood of Christ" during Communion were engaging in cannibalism.

In our own era it is primarily tantric practices (such as breath control, meditation, kriya and mantra yogas), not orthodox Brahminism, that have been transplanted from India to Western culture. It is still nearly impossible for an Indian woman growing up in a traditional brahmin household to receive initiation in the Gayatri mantra, while nearly any sincere American student can drive to a nearby yoga center and be given the Gayatri. This is due to Tantra's central tenet of *adhikara,* "worthiness." According to the tantric adepts, worthiness is a matter of the heart, not of one's class, sex, or nationality.

In Lalla's time, the tantric tradition was particularly strong in Kashmir. Sri Siddhanath, deeply impressed by Lalla's *adhikara,* initiated her in the mysteries of the thirty-six *tattvas* (elements), showing her how to shift her awareness from the physical elements to those states of subtle matter that exist only in the mind. From there he taught her how to direct her consciousness to even more subtle levels beyond the grasp of ordinary human mentation. According to legend, he helped her pierce the five *kanchukas* or limiting conditions that separate human awareness from divine being: the illusion that there is anything we cannot accomplish; the illusion that there is anything we do not know; the illusion that anything exists outside ourselves which in turn gives birth to desire; the illusion that we are limited by causation; and the illusion that space separates one object from another. Tantrics believe that in the deepest states of meditation one can experience existence as Shiva himself does: as unlimited awareness and creative power.

In the oral tradition of India it is said that one thing pleases the guru more than any other: a disciple whose spiritual achievement grows to exceed the guru's own. Lalleshvari was such a disciple. The depth of her wisdom amazed her contemporaries, including Siddhanath himself. The most impressive factor was that the root of her insight lay not in "book learning" as did that of so many scholars of the day, but in her own meditative experience. Lalla was afire with spiritual knowledge, but it was the light of spirit, not the brilliance of intellect, that shone through her. Calling on the force of her own realization, Lalla was easily able to defeat learned pandits who came to debate with her. To this day Lalleshvari is acknowledged as one of the greatest masters of Kashmir Shaivism who ever lived.

"Instead of allowing others to serve you, learn to serve," Lalla advised the arrogant pandits who challenged her. "Humility is a sign of greatness.

"Meditate on the divinity within yourself. Drink the nectar of love that continually pours from the heart of God."

Gazing up at the glaciers crowning the mountains of Kashmir, Lalla taught, "Water freezes into ice, and ice—grazed by the sun's rays—melts again into water. Just so, all pervading consciousness congeals into this ephemeral material universe. But when matter is grazed by the compassionate glance of God, it releases itself once more into all pervasive being.

"In the vast and pure being of Shiva, the drama of life and death is staged. People do not understand that this is all the play of the Goddess Consciousness herself."

Lalla pointed out that although there is someone inside us who "drowns" in deep sleep, there is someone or something deeper that remains awake. It is by discovering that One Who Never Sleeps that we find our true Self.

Like Mahadevi, Lalleshvari freed herself from social restraints and travelled through India as an *avadhut*, a yogini established in states of awareness far beyond consensus reality. Whether she was dressed or not, whether she ate or not, whether others respected or mocked her, were not her concerns. "I abide in the totality, and the totality abides in me." Her devotees claim that when she finally died, she simply dissolved in light.

The vast majority of India's women saints led far less dramatic lives, usually within the context of family life. From the dawn of history, remarkable women like Arundhati (circa 4000 B.C.E.) were hailed by the Vedas themselves as wives and mothers who achieved Self realization while cleaning their homes and raising their children. One notable modern example is Anasuya Devi, born in Andhra Pradesh in 1923. From early childhood Anasuya's astute observations on spiritual topics—even subjects as recondite as the *mantra shastra* (science of mantras)—astonished her elders; she seemed a spiritual prodigy. No world-abnegating ascetic, Anasuya was pleased to marry. At the age of eighteen she left her well-to-do brahmin parents to move in with the husband they had selected for her, Nannagaru Rao, and cheerfully began to raise a family in the poor South Indian town of Jillellamudi. She would remain deeply devoted to Nannagaru (whose interest in spirituality was significantly less than hers) throughout her life.

Anasuya was twenty-six when she met her "guru," Desiraju Rajamma, a woman teacher of both Vedantic philosophy and Tantra practice who lived in Bapatla. Anasuya's aunt arranged the meeting, feeling that a young woman with such a strong spiritual streak should receive a mantra initiation. At the initiation, however, Rajamma was so impressed by the depth of Anasuya's realization that she sent for a photographer to take their picture together so that she would have a momento of this first meeting with her "disciple"!

"What a remarkable woman you are!" the would-be guru exclaimed.

"I am the woman who gave birth to you, and you are the woman who gave birth to me," Anasuya replied. "Who is the mother and who is not the mother? Real motherhood does not consist in the simple recognition of one's own motherhood. Motherhood must be perceived in everything." As Rajamma recognized, Anasuya was referring to the motherhood of God. A meditator since childhood, Anasuya had already discovered the Universal Mother in herself, and in all beings.

While Nannagaru worked as the village officer, Anasuya organized a grain bank to help feed the poor. In the early 1950s, word began to spread to nearby villages that a "divine being" lived in Jillellamudi, and devotees started showing up at Anasuya's house, which was soon aptly rechristened "the Home of All." Nannagaru was initially uncomfortable with all the attention his wife was attracting, and at one point summoned a doctor to examine her. While Anasuya sat smiling at him, the physician was unable to locate a pulse anywhere in her body. "I find more *yoga* (union with God) than *roga* (disease) in her," he stated, savvy enough to diagnose *sahaja samadhi* (deep meditative absorption while moving about in the waking state). After that Nannagaru began calling Anasuya "your Mother" rather than "my wife" when devotees appeared to see her.

At one point Anasuya notified Dr. Sitachalam of Kommur that she would be going on an eleven-day journey. Would he please look after her body and ensure that no one removed it? The doctor was present when she "left." Her heartbeat and respiration ceased, and her body froze in a blue-gray pallor. By the fourth day her distraught family was ready to cremate her, but the physician anxiously insisted they delay. On the eleventh day color returned to her cheeks, and she rose from her cot to resume her household chores.

In the past few decades, scientific studies at laboratories both in India and in the West have confirmed that advanced yogis and yoginis can assume such states of "suspended animation" for at least short periods (so that they can travel unhampered by their physical bodies, the mystics claim). What is unusual in Anasuya's case is that she appears to have mastered the technique without having been taught.

In Shaivite Tantra, the highest state of unalloyed, contentless awareness (Shiva, the supreme Godhead) is simultaneously the brimming consciousness/power (Shakti, the primordial Goddess) which manifests as the universe and all its denizens. Anasuya directly experienced Shakti and spoke from the perspective of mystical union with the Mother of the Universe. "I am turning the whole world over in my mind. I am experiencing that my one mind has become the many. Reality itself is my state. Adopt me as your child and in one step you will become the grandparent of the whole creation.

"I am not anything that you are not. It doesn't appear to me that I am greater than you. God does not exist separately anywhere. You are all God.

"It is not correct to say 'Mother of the Universe.' The universe itself is the mother. You can never fall from my lap."

Anasuya was not at all interested in being worshiped, nor in prescribing spiritual practices for her devotees to follow. There was nothing they must "do," they were simply to "be." She experienced herself and everyone around her as redolent with divinity. Not through any effort on their own part, but only through the grace of Shakti herself could others also relax back into their own essence and experience this too.

The question of how one comes into mystical unity with the Mother of the Universe was an urgent concern for Hyma, Anasuya's daughter. Hyma would cry herself to sleep at night because she could see the divine state glimmering in her mother's eyes, but she could not experience it herself. Though her humility and service endeared her to her mother's devotees, many of whom believed she would take her mother's place as their spiritual guide after Anasuya's passing, Hyma was deeply frustrated. "Could I, dear Mother, ever attain that state where my consciousness will be filled with you and you alone?" she wrote in a letter. "This is the anguish of my heart." Many souls have sensed the enormous gulf between their own experience and that of a God-realized sage, but the crisis was intensely acute for Hyma, since the sage in question was her own biological mother!

A devotee recorded a particularly poignant conversation between Hyma and her mother. "With such a fickle mind as I have, can I ever achieve Self realization?"

"I don't know anything about achieving goals."

"Yes Mother, you are yourself the goal so you don't need to think about it! But the rest of us must strive and find a way to reach there."

"Well, for me, there is joy in the game and the mischief done," Anasuya smiled.

A devotee interrupted that watching the mischief was more fun than doing penance but Hyma persisted, "Please stop evading the question! I need an answer! We are not like you. From our point of view the path, the effort, and the spiritual goal are completely real!"

The verbal jousting continued, playful on the part of the mother, deadly earnest on the part of the daughter. Anasuya artfully dodged Hyma's pleas, but finally quietly concluded, "There is no need to tell a lie. You will become the reality itself."

Hyma was an extremely sensitive girl. After she saw a bird's nest fall to the ground, destroying the eggs inside it, Hyma could not eat for a week. Suffering affected her deeply, and she gave of herself continuously in an effort to help. Her body felt the toll as her health collapsed.

Hyma was twenty-five when she became critically ill with smallpox. Friends wished to rush her to the hospital in Guntur, but Anasuya demurred, explaining that the difficult ride would only aggravate the condition. Anasuya was overruled as neighbors and relatives became increasingly frantic and a car was hired. Hyma died a few minutes after arriving at the hospital. At the last moment of her life she called out loudly, "Amma [Mother], I am coming!"

The Jillellamudi community was extremely shaken by Hyma's death. Was even Anasuya, the embodiment of the Shakti herself, not exempt from such personal tragedy? "I made the dagger, and with that dagger I stabbed myself," Anasuya soberly replied, as ever mystically identified with the Goddess.

A *samadhi* shrine (mausoleum) was prepared for Hyma. (In India, saints are sometimes buried rather than cremated, so that devotees can continue to experience the uplifting vibrations emanating from their bodies even after they have died.) Anasuya cleaned the body and placed it in the samadhi pit in *siddhasana* (a yoga posture). While the entire community stood by weeping, Anasuya seemed strangely cheerful. She sat beside the grave and smiled at the onlookers. "If I sit like this, people may think I am transmitting power," she joked. Then she signalled to a doctor standing nearby. He examined Hyma's body and was shocked to find it quite hot, with a faint trace of respiration. He had just climbed out of the pit when the group standing nearby felt an electric jolt. He leapt back into the grave and discovered blood oozing from Hyma's fontanel. In the scriptures of yoga, it is written that at death an open fontanel is a sign that the soul has left the body through the *sahasrara chakra,* the "divine exit" at the top of the head, and become liberated.

"My work is finished," Anasuya said as she walked away from the grave.

§

In addition to historical saints, women of spirit appear throughout the mystical literature of India. Several are described in the *Tripura Rahasya* (Mystery of the Triune Goddess), one of the major texts of Shaktism, the ancient Indian Goddess tradition. There is, for example, the story of the princess who spiritually awakened an entire kingdom.

Prince Hemachuda was hunting deep in the forest when a ferocious windstorm separated him from the rest of his party. Struggling against the powerful gusts, he glimpsed a small hermitage through the swirling clouds of dust. A young woman greeted him at the door, and welcomed him hospitably with fruit and juice.

Hemachuda could not take his eyes off the woman. A clarity and intelligence radiated from her that was completedly unlike the silly and superficial girls at court. "Who are you?" he demanded. "Why are you living here alone in the forest?"

The woman smilingly explained that her name was Hemalekha. She was the foster daughter of the sage Vyaghrapada. Together she and her father lived quietly in the forest, practicing yoga and worshiping Shiva.

When the winds died down Vyaghrapada returned home, and the love-smitten Hemachuda asked for his permission to marry Hemalekha. With his clairvoyant powers Vyaghrapada looked into the future, and seeing that only good would come of this union, gladly gave his consent.

Hemachuda threw himself enthusiastically into married life, but noted that his wife never lost a certain reserve. While her wit, playfulness, and obvious love for him delighted the prince, he was confused by the dispassion that seemed to underlie her actions. "I am always looking up to you, like a lily turning its face to the moon, but nothing I do seems to please you," he complained one day. "Here at the palace you are surrounded by the greatest pleasures life has to offer, yet you seem unmoved by them. Why are you so indifferent to the wonderful things I can offer?"

"Darling, it's not that I don't love you," Hemalekha answered. "But I'm searching for the greatest joy of all, pleasure that will never lose its flavor. All the delightful things I've experienced here become tiresome after a while. Happiness is relative, and depends on our attitude toward objects and events at the time. Right now my body appears beautiful to you, but as I get older, will it continue to appeal to you? Everything we cherish in life is eventually taken away from us, even our own bodies. There is no lasting happiness here."

As Hemalekha spoke of the transience and sorrow of the world, Hemachuda found dispassion beginning to well up in his mind too. As the months passed, Hemachuda felt himself in a psychological wasteland, one moment surrendering to his old impulses to indulge himself, and at the next feeling disgusted with himself and with people and things that no longer seemed to satisfy him. Finally he got on his horse and rode out to an old, abandoned tower. Ensconcing himself in the highest room, he sat down to follow his wife's detailed instructions about meditation and find lasting peace within himself.

As the weeks went by, Hemachuda's meditation deepened until finally he reached *nirvikalpa samadhi,* the deepest state in which duality vanishes and one is immersed in the absolute unity of pure being. The experience dumbfounded the prince, who had never imagined such bliss existed, and he determined to spend the rest of his life in this condition.

One day Hemachuda felt his wife sitting quietly beside him, but he refused to open his eyes. "I pity you," he said, "still going through the motions of life at court. I have found the greatest good and will remain here in perfect Self realization. I wish you well, but please leave me alone."

"Darling, you are still as far from Self realization as the reflection of the stars in a pool is from the sky," Hemalekha smiled. "What kind of realization is this that vanishes the moment you open your eyes? Abide in your true Self—the consciousness in which all this universe manifests like an image on the surface of a mirror—and resume your responsibilities at court. The Self is not harmed if you leave the world or if you remain in it, if you work or if you refuse to work, if you reject me or if you care for me. My dearest love, come home."

Hemachuda's father and brothers were amazed at the difference in him. He now went about administering the kingdom with tranquility and wisdom, and his relationshipship with his bride had changed from one of passionate infatuation to profound respect and deep sharing. When his relations asked Hemachuda how he had come to change so much, he taught them just as Hemalekha had taught him. Now the ministers were impressed at the dramatic change in the royal family, who were suddenly showing a maturity and serenity completely uncharacteristic of them. The king then taught the ministers how to find peace in themselves. And now the people of the kingdom could scarcely believe the transformation in their ministers, who were suddenly tempering their actions with spiritual insight. The people wanted to know how this had happened, and the ministers in turn taught them.

In the end nothing at all changed: Hemachuda and Hemalekha still loved each other, the king still ruled, the ministers still ministered, the washermen still cleaned the laundry, the cooks still cooked, even the prostitutes still entertained clients. But everything had changed: all the people went about their business with Self awareness and a profound mutual respect born from their newfound recognition that the divine being they had discovered in themselves also existed in every other living thing.

Sitting alone in his forest hermitage, Vyaghrapada smiled. His daughter had done well.

Another popular story about a woman sage who leads her husband to the highest states of awareness—and back again—occurs in the mystical masterpiece, *Yoga Vashishtha.* King Sikhidhvaja and Queen Chudala were very happily married. While the king was off attending to royal affairs, however, Chudala began to wonder about the nature of consciousness. "I do not believe I am my body, for the principle of intelligence inside myself directs the body as a bat directs the motion of a ball. And yet this inner intelligence disappears in sleep and in deep meditation like a flame immersed in water. What am I then?" Plunging within, Chudala eventually discovered the undying Self. "I have found the imperishable One, the one thing truly worth knowing!" she exclaimed.

Sikhidhvaja noted the remarkable transformation in his wife: she had become luminescent. But when Chudala tried to find words to express the state she was experiencing, Sikhidhvaja just laughed. He could not believe that this woman whom he had known since childhood could actually have reached such a level of yogic mastery. Chudala gave up trying to share her experience with her husband, and relapsed into the role of wife and lover while continuing to secretly enjoy extraordinary adventures in consciousness. The text says that she "passed effortlessly through fire and wood and stone, skimmed over the mountain peaks, and communicated freely with animals, with savage tribes, and with the gods."

As he got older, the king's mind turned to philosophy. Seeing his body aging, he decided it was time to renounce the world and seek enlightenment. Leaving his wife to rule the kingdom, Sikhidhvaja retired deep into the forest to practice severe asceticism. Chudala was disappointed to see him go, especially since she didn't believe he had the spiritual maturity to truly benefit from the penance he chose to undergo. From time to time she would leave her body in the palace and fly out to check on her husband. Watching Sikhidhvaja getting thinner and weaker as he fanatically continued his ascetic practices made Chudala very sad.

Chudala was a passionate woman, and the years without her husband's company were difficult for her. Sometimes as she traveled through the other universes that coexist with our own, she would see the women *siddhas* (perfected masters) moving through the sky on their way to rendevouz with their sage husbands. This always made her wistful.

After eighteen years, Chudala sensed that it was time to act. Sikhidhvaja was finally beginning to realize that going through the motions of spiritual practice was not getting him anywhere. He was finally ready to accept the guidance of an enlightened guru, but the queen knew he was still not ready for a woman guru, especially if the woman was his own wife. So she approached him disguised as a young male ascetic named Kumbha.

Sikhidhvaja was instantly attracted to Kumbha, who reminded him of the wife he had loved long ago. Kumbha's *tejas* (spiritual radiance) deeply affected the former king. He had been able to dismiss that luminosity when he saw it in his wife decades earlier, but seeing it now in this young boy the king recognized it for what it was: the aura of enlightenment.

After talking together for some time, Sikhidhvaja confessed, "I strictly observe all the prescribed rituals daily without fail, and I have mortified my body severely, but I have achieved nothing spiritually. To tell the truth, all that I've gotten from my years of penance is depressed!"

"And do you wish to continue your present practice, dwelling in the forest and eating roots, struggling to forsake the evil tendencies of your mind, while living like an insect in a hole in the ground?" Kumbha challenged mercilessly. "It's time for you to stop play-acting at spirituality, and engage in authentic spiritual self-inquiry. What is the universe and what is your place in it? Who are you? These are the questions you should be asking. You should seek out the company of the wise, so that they can guide you to the answers."

"Please be my guru," Sikhidhvaja pleaded. "Share with me the knowledge of how I may free myself from sorrow. Show me how to find that everlasting bliss the scriptures speak about!"

Just as *Tripura Rahasya* details Hemalekha's teachings at great length, the *Yoga Vashishtha* devotes many chapters to the sage Chudala's instructions to her husband. She led him to see that the universe is actually not material at all, and cannot be said to have either a beginning or an end. In reality it is a figment in the limitless consciousness of God. By directing him to continuously ask "Who am I?" Chudala helped the king strip away the layers of illusion in his own life, including his body and the perturbations in his mind, to find his divine core, coeval with God. The shock of God realization was so profound that Sikhidhvaja entered a catatonic state for three days, barely breathing. To prevent him from losing his grip on his body entirely, Chudala entered his mind and jarred him back to the waking state.

Chudala was more than ready to resume her marriage but, having taken her husband to the heights of mystical experience, now had to find a gentle way to bring him back to earth. Still disguised as the ascetic boy Kumbha, Chudala claimed she had been cursed by the irascible sage Durvasa to become a woman at night. Resuming a female form each evening, Chudala attempted to seduce the king, but he was still so immersed in inner bliss that he remained oblivious to her charms. Finally she convinced him that there was nothing wrong with following the dictates of nature, and induced Sikhidhvaja to marry Kumbha, the boy-by-day/girl-by-night. The king sincerely loved Kumbha and accepted him/her as friend and lover, but nothing disturbed his equanimity.

Chudala/Kumbha arranged several more tests for the king: offering him all the pleasures of heaven, and letting him find her in the arms of another lover. He was not moved by either greed or jealousy. Delighted by her student's progress, Chudala at last revealed her true identity to the king. Sikhidhvaja, who had matured considerably since the days when he could not believe his wife could be a yogic adept, was overjoyed to discover that his beloved Chudala had been his guru all along.

"There is one thing I must ask of you," Chudala announced.

"You have been the most gracious wife in the world," Sikhidhvaja answered gratefully. "I will do whatever you request."

"You won't like it, dear."

"If there's one thing I've learned it's that nothing that happens externally, 'good' or 'bad,' can disturb me so long as I abide in my true nature, the Self."

"Then return home, and rule your kingdom."

"What!"

"Darling, the world may be a figment in the mind of God, but we all have a role to play in God's drama. Even enlightened men and women must fulfill their duties in the world. You have an obligation to your people. Come home, and govern your people wisely."

The text concludes that Sikhidhvaja and Chudala ruled together for over a thousand years. When their responsibilities had been fulfilled, they left their bodies together and vanished forever into the ineffable vastness of the refulgent mind of God.

As I leaf through the pages of Indian history, or sit in Hindu homes listening to tales of woman saints immortalized in the oral tradition, I wonder what it might have been like growing up not with Cinderella or Sleeping Beauty as role models, but Lalleshvari or Mira Bai. Suppose, instead of aspiring to be presidents of software firms, ultra thin models, or successful artists and scholars, we women of the West could also picture ourselves as divine beings who moved at will through the inner corridors of the universe? What if a wise old woman had taught us not only about mastering a profession or a social role, but about mastering ourselves? What if we had grown up knowing we were daughters of the Goddess?

Chudala and Hemalekha were conceived by a culture that honors women of spirit as much as we value professional basketball players and Oscar winners in ours. No wonder our fantasy women marry princes and live happily ever after while theirs marry princes, cultivate wisdom, and discover in themselves the essence of all things. While the traditional social role of women in India has been even more narrow than in the West, India's conception of what it means to be a "liberated woman" is infinitely broader. After studying with Pandit Rajmani and his radiant wife I found myself backpacking through South Asia, hoping to learn what the wise women of Asia can teach us, their sisters and brothers on the other side of the world.

CONTEMPORARY
HINDU
WOMEN SAINTS

"*T*here are many great women saints in India," Pandit Rajmani assured me. Who are they? What do they teach? How do they live? Looking for answers, I set out to meet some of the great Indian women masters of our own day, leaders who form the crest of a new wave of spiritual energy that is flooding not only the East but the parched continents of the Western world as well.

Indian women have actually always been the backbone of Hindu religious life. Unlike most Western faiths, which are celebrated communally once each week, Hinduism is usually practiced daily in the home. Morning and evening worship before the family altar is often conducted by the women of the house, and the numerous legends that illustrate Hinduism's highest principles have been passed—in some cases for thousands of years—primarily from mother to child.

It is no accident that in India the deity who governs education, the arts, and religious knowledge is Sarasvati; the deity associated with strength and protection is Durga; the deity who rules wealth and commerce is Lakshmi—all are Goddesses. I am trying to remember a time when I walked into an Indian home or business and did not find the portrait of at least one of these Goddesses hanging on the wall; I honestly cannot recall a single instance. While we in Europe and America decorate our homes with pictures of ourselves and our relatives, Indians surround themselves with portraits of divinity, constant reminders of the spiritual dimension of life and the compassionate motherhood of God. Today, as social strictures against women continue to crumble, more than ever Indian women are free not only to worship the goddesses but to imitate them, both in the home and on the world stage.

In the past century, some of India's foremost spiritual giants have acted to redress a seeming gender imbalance in their tradition, even when it has meant coaxing reluctant female disciples into the limelight. One after another, major Indian teachers have passed their spiritual mantle to women disciples.

Early in the 1900's the controversial tantric adept, Upasani Baba, reinstituted the Vedic tradition of *kanyadin,* a sort of Hindu convent, and encouraged women to practice Vedic rites without the supervision of male priests. He taught that women are capable of faster spiritual evolution than men, and that male devotees needed to cultivate "feminine" qualities like egolessness and purity in order to progress. He passed his lineage to the late Godavari Mataji, who presided over the Kanya Kumari Sthan in Sakori.

Ramakrishna (world renowned devotee of the goddess Kali) passed his spiritual authority to his wife, Sarada Devi; Paramahansa Yogananda (who carried the Kriya Yoga lineage to the West) to the American-born Daya Mata; Shivananda (yogi and prolific author of Rishikesh) to the Canadian Shivananda Radha; Swami Paramananda (the first swami to settle in America) to his niece, Gayatri Devi; Swami Lakshmana (one of the peerless Ramana Maharshi's premier disciples) to the rebellious young Mathru Sri Sarada; Dhyanyogi Madhusudandas (long-lived exponent of kundalini yoga) to Anandi Ma; and Swami Muktananda (world travelling ambassador of Siddha Yoga) to Gurumayi Chidvilasananda.

Papa Ramdas, one of the most homey of the popular Indian saints of this century, shared his mission with his spiritual consort, Krishna Bai. Sri Aurobindo, the influential philosopher/saint of Pondicherry, deferred to the French woman Mirra Alfassa Richard, whom he called "The Mother" and who administered Auroville, the community he founded in India, after his passing. Meera Ma (born in 1960 in Chandepalle, Andhra Pradesh), who had visions of Aurobindo since her childhood, has moved to Germany where European students have given her a warm welcome. Her legend continues to grow. And to everyone's surprise, the arch conservative shankaracharya of Sringeri empowered a woman (Lakshmi Devi

Ashram, Jewish by birth) to found the first American temple to the
Divine Mother in Stroudsburg, Pennsylvania.

Also during this century Indian women have taken great
strides in empowering themselves spiritually. When Anandamayi
Ma, one of the most extraordinary women of all time, could not
find a pandit willing to give her a mantra, she initiated herself.
Anasuya Devi realized her unity with the Goddess without the aid of
a guru, as did Amritanandamayi Ma. Brahmajna Ma, widowed at
age ten, self-enlightened at thirty-two, explained, "He alone can
realize the Self without a guru's help in whose mind arise questions
such as, 'Who am I, what is the world, where was I before, and
where shall I go? Where is peace?'"

Indian women have often had to face tremendous obstacles
in order to fulfill their spiritual destinies. Women's status in Indian
civilization is a complex subject, and varies considerably not only
from class to class and era to era, but sometimes from one village
to another. India is actually a patched quilt of many different
languages and cultures, some rabidly patriarchal (due in part,
paradoxically, to the need to protect women during Moghul and
Turkic incursions), some overtly matriarchal. To be fair, men didn't
always have it easy either, even in the spiritually charged atmosphere of India. Many of South Asia's most respected male seers,
including Ramakrishna, Ramana Maharshi, Adi Shankaracharya,
and even the Buddha, fought enormous familial pressure to aban-
don their spiritual preoccupations and settle down to more
normative lifestyles.

Yet even within the context of a generally male dominated
system, women have often risen to roles of spiritual preeminence.
Several episodes from the life of Adi Shankaracharya (who flourished, according to Western scholars, in the 9th century A.D.) may
help to illustrate this. Shankaracharya was considered one of the
two greatest Hindu philosopher/saints of that era. The other was
his nemesis Mandana Mishra, so when they two finally met to
debate, scholars converged to watch and record the battle of the
century. The stakes were high: whoever lost would have to become
the disciple of the other. There was, however, one significant
tactical problem that had to be resolved before the event could
begin: if these were the two leading thinkers of their time, who was
qualified to evaluate their arguments and declare a winner?

Shankara and Mandana agreed the only individual both
intelligent and impartial enough to serve as judge was Bharati
Mishra, Mandana's erudite wife. Shankaracharya defeated
Mandana in several days, but when Bharati herself asked him to

debate, Shankara had to request a six month recess while he pondered her challenging theses about spiritual life. Shankara won this debate too—just barely—but was so impressed by Bharati's sanctity that he named one of his monastic orders after her.

You may believe you have never heard of Shankaracharya, but the odds are that you or someone you know has been influenced by his thought. Shankara was one of the first yogis to widely publicize the idea that the world is all *maya,* an illusion, and that we are in reality all one. He was one of the most influential thinkers in Asian history. For most of his life, though, he discounted the feminine principle, considering anything to do with matter or desire a lower order of being.

One day late in his short life, as he was entering a Shiva temple, he found an hysterical low-caste woman blocking his way. She was standing over the corpse of her dead husband, sobbing wildly. Shankara found the scene both distasteful and inauspicious. "Get out of my way!" he commanded.

The illiterate woman looked at him suspiciously. "Aren't you the teacher who says that everything is Brahman, everything is God, there is no impurity anywhere?" she retorted bitterly. "If I am not impure, why should I get out of your way? If I am the all pervading reality, how *can* I get out of your way?"

Shankara was too shocked to reply.

The woman was not done with him. "Your mighty Brahman is no more than this!" she shouted, pointing to her dead husband.

In that moment the great thinker's mind burst open. He remembered one of the most dramatic images from India's vast religious iconography: the raging goddess Kali stamping on the corpse of the God Shiva. Without Her power, Shiva himself is not able to stir, say the Shaktas, the worshippers of the Goddess. In that fraction of a second, Shankara realized that in neglecting the Goddess, he had missed the very essence of life. Imagining Brahman as totally abstract, unalloyed, unmoving consciousness, he had forgotten the fecund, creative, active, living aspect of reality, the feminine. Now Kali herself was manifesting to remind him of her glory.

To the horror of his disciples, Shankaracharya got down on his knees and clasped the woman's feet, thanking her for the lesson. "No you are not impure. It was my mind that was impure. I have never met a greater teacher than you."

Shankara gave up writing philosophy and spent the last few years of his life composing ecstatic poems to the Goddess, some of which are still regarded as among the most beautiful verses in the Sanskrit language.

Women of extraordinary insight, whether feted like Bharati Mishra or anonymous like the grieving outcaste widow, have made their indelible imprint on Indian spirituality in the millennia since Shankara, with or without the approbation of society. Similar women walk the soil of India today. Some tend their families in rural villages unreachable by any paved road. Some study, or teach, in the universities. Some live invisibly in forest shacks and mountain crevices.

An example of these invisible saints is Maya Amma, a yogini perhaps eighty years old, well known in southwest India but rarely seen. Maya Amma is an *avadhut,* a radically unconventional sage who, like Akka Mahadevi, has completely renounced the world. She does not bother about any of the material concerns that absorb the attention of the rest of us, including clothing, and wanders the jungle near Cape Cocoran clad only in the sky. She doesn't teach; in fact it's rare to hear her speak at all. No one knows where she came from, only that she travels capriciously across the southern tip of India surrounded by a pack of half-wild dogs. Some of the greatest saints of India have made pilgrimages to her feet.

Maya Amma is what the tantras calls a *madhya* type of yogini. This is a soul who has gone so far beyond body awareness that only the thinnest thread of consciousness maintains a connection with the physical brain. Thus its last few vestigates of karma are played out through the body while the soul's awareness remains merged in the absolute. (Muktananda's guru Nityananda was this type of yogi.)

Increasingly, however, India's women saints preside over ashrams, sharing their wisdom with the thousands who flock to see and hear them. It will be interesting to observe over the next few decades if they manage to retain their balance under the onslaught of television cameras, uncritical devotion, and large donations. Perhaps the technology and comparative wealth we admirers from the West bring with us will constitute the most serious test of integrity India's women of spirit have faced.

I would like to introduce you to some of these remarkable women. I have deliberately focused on saints who are very accessible: whom you can meet, if you choose to. (The exception is Anandamayi Ma, who left our world in 1982. She had such an enormous impact on the course of women's spirituality in India however, that it was impossible to exclude her. She in effect became the standard against which Indian women of spirit will be compared for centuries to come.)

If you have never studied with an Indian teacher before, you are in for some surprises. These women embody a spiritual tradition radically different from the Judaic, Christian, and Islamic religions of the West. Not only in their thought, but in their experience, divinity is not a stern father who created the world and judges it from above, salvaging some souls and eternally condemning others, but is the matrix of the universe, an unlimited awareness that underlies and permeates all things. It may be anthropomorphized as a father, but also (as by Mira Bai) as a lover, (as by Anasuya) as a mother, or as any other form or concept that carries us emotionally toward the source and end of our own being. From this perspective no one is condemned, except perhaps by the force of their own misguided judgment. God is not someone one learns about in church on Sundays, but something one feels in one's own heart (perhaps most clearly during deep meditation) and honors in all one's fellow beings. Goddess is not a political symbol of self empowerment, but the way the cosmos treats its sentient children: like a mother, like a jealous lover, like a playful little girl.

Indian women saints should not be confused with the women of power of shamanic traditions, even though the tantric worldview certainly has shamanic roots. To a great extent the shamanic journey is an exploration of humanity's collective subconscious. Yogic culture sidesteps this dimension of human experience to a large degree—for better or worse—focusing instead on what, for lack of a better term, might be called the superconscious. Power, self affirmation, and celebration of earth energy are not the goal: conscious immersion in a reality that precedes earth and ego is more to the point. Because of this divergence of emphasis the teachings of Indian's women of spirit are to some degree out of sync with the present evocation of Goddess energy in the West. What we think of as the Goddess here would be considered merely a strand or two of her hair in South Asia, where women have had over 10,000 continuous years to get to know her intimately. These women have cultivated a vision that includes ecstatic love but also rigorous self-discipline, self discovery but also selfless service. They are interested not so much in the dream time as in the dreamer.

If you are inspired to go and sit in the presence of these saints, you will meet women who have overcome far worse social barriers than we women experience in the West, probably than we can even honestly imagine. You will meet women steeped from birth in a religion incredibly ancient long before our own Western

faiths were even formulated, and therefore holding an extraordinarily different perspective about life, about personal responsibility, and
about human potential. You may be inspired, you may be
displeased, you may simply be perplexed, but your own vision about
who you are and what you can be will definitely be challenged.

Incidently, most churches, synagogues and mosques remain
opposed to female clergy. Yet the burgeoning prominence of
women in the Indian spiritual tradition no longer strikes observers
as unusual, and is quickly moving toward the norm. Perhaps as we
once adopted yoga and meditation from the East, we will also learn
to value feminine leadership in spirituality, inspired by the example
of the liberated women of India.

SRI MA OF KAMAKHYA: LIVING THE GODDESS

The Mother of the Universe is flying to Bengal. The folds of her white sari flutter around her like wings. For seven years she has been doing rigorous penance, ministering to the spiritually impoverished in a remote region called America. Now at last she is returning to India.

A huge crowd has gathered outside Dum Dum Airport to welcome her home. *"Jai Ma!"* (Victory to the Mother of the Universe!) the devotees roar as they watch her jet taxi into the international concourse. "Do they mean hail to the Goddess, or to Sri Ma?" I whisper to my husband.

"I don't think they make that distinction," Johnathan whispers back.

Sri Ma steps off the plane, obviously in no hurry. She finds a seat in the airport's bleak concrete lounge while friends run off to attend to her luggage—dozens of large, taped cardboard boxes filled with clothing from America to distribute to the poor. Some of Calcutta's leading citizens, who have used their political stature to circumvent the armed guards at the concourse entrance, rush forward to place their heads reverently at her feet.

At first glance, Sri Ma is an unlikely Goddess. There is no aura of command about her; she is so humble I might have imagined she was the servant of one of the prosperous Indian devotees. I have read a great deal about the cultivation of egolessness, but nothing could have prepared me for the experience of actually being in the presence of pure selflessness. Sri Ma was completely transparent, almost invisible. There was no agitation in her whatsoever; it was almost as if the air itself was not disturbed when she passed by.

It's hard to believe this simple woman of indeterminate age is the daughter of one of the wealthiest and most respected families in north India, that she once lived in a mansion, waited on by a bevy of servants herself. She was sixteen when she wandered off into the forest, abandoning a life of luxury to completely immerse herself in all-pervading divinity. Her parents conducted a frantic nationwide search, not yet willing to concede they had lost their daughter to God.

Johnathan, who is a veteran traveler to South Asia, grins at me as Sri Ma and the mass of beaming devotees pile into the tank-like Hindustani Ambassador cabs waiting outside the airport. He has some advice for me before we head into Bengal and Bihar, the Goddess' ancient stomping grounds. "Don't think of this as being in another country. Think of it as being on another planet. Everything in India is totally different, even the laws of physics. Things that should work, don't. Things that can't happen, do."

I am curious to visit a culture where the Universal Mother has been honored continuously since prehistory. We will be traveling with Sri Ma, one of northeastern India's best loved saints, herself a devotee of the Goddess—and, in India, where even the laws of physics are different, whom some would call the Goddess herself.

§

I first met Sri Ma at the Devi Mandir (Sanskrit for Goddess Temple) she founded in California. The temple was not unlike the TARDIS, Dr. Who's phone booth-shaped spaceship: tiny and non-descript outside, spacious and brimming with surprises within. Walking in the door was like stepping through a space warp: I felt as if I'd set foot in India. Portraits of saints and deities from all religious traditions, reflecting the broadly ecumenical spirit of Hinduism, covered the walls like wallpaper. In the middle of the room was a huge firepit, flames aroar, into which a swami cast handfuls of rice and barley as he chanted the names of the Goddess.

At the front of the temple was an enormous altar, peopled by a dozen beautifully robed plaster idols of the Divine Mother. Some of them were benign; others, like the ferocious warrior Goddess Kali, seemed threatening with their upraised weapons and menacing eyes. They were all characters from the *Chandi*, India's most sacred Goddess text, which recounts the exploits of the

Universal Mother when she manifested to destroy the demon Mahisha. The text is an elaborate allegory of the purifying effect of expanded spiritual awareness on human egotism. The *Chandi* was chanted here daily, a ritual that took from two to four hours, depending on the singer's pace.

Sri Ma was nowhere to be seen, which surprised me since I had heard she had not left the premises in years; she had taken a vow to remain in the temple until the *Chandi* has been celebrated a thousand times. Finally a young American woman in a sari directed me to the kitchen where Sri Ma was preparing dinner for her devotees. I was taken aback; I have visited many ashrams throughout the United States and am used to devotees waiting hand and foot on their guru. A guru who waits on her devotees was a new experience.

Ma's complexion was very dark, not unlike Kali's. She was short and thin, frail looking, but uncannily graceful. Her wavy black hair streamed freely to her waist. She was somewhat wall-eyed, so that it was difficult to tell whether she was looking at me or past me. This impression of being here and elsewhere at the same time was one I would become familiar with as I got to know Ma.

Sri Ma was not interested in talking about herself. "Linda, how are you? Will you stay for the *Chandi?*" Her voice was high and musical, underscoring her Indian style femininity. Then she resumed her kitchen chores, wrapped in an aura of shimmering silence. She reminded me of a small bird, light and delicate, ready to spring into the air at any moment.

Sri Ma came to the United States in 1984 at the request of her guru, Ramakrishna Paramahansa. This was a startling command, particularly since Ramakrishna died sixty years before Sri Ma was born. From earliest girlhood, however, Sri Ma felt close to the nineteenth century Bengali saint, sensing that her inner guidance emanated from him. Westerners may smile but an orthodox Hindu would not have a problem with this sort of belief; during his lifetime Ramakrishna was recognized by some of the greatest religious leaders of India as an incarnation of God. In 1892, six years after his death, he appeared to his disciple Swami Vivekananda, instructing him to take the Vedantic understanding of the innate divinity of humanity and the equal value of all religions to the West. Vivekananda was the first Hindu to widely present the *sanatana dharma,* the eternal truth of the Vedas, in the occident. His spectacularly successful debut at the World Congress of Religions in Chicago in 1893 led to the founding of numerous Vedanta centers throughout the North America and Europe, many of which are still active. Ramakrishna's directions to Sri Ma were equally explicit: Go to the West. Serve the devotees.

Ironically, America of the 1980's was less receptive to Ramakrishna's initiative than the America of the 1890's. Sri Ma attempted to open temples devoted to worship of the Divine Mother in several small American communities but in each instance hostile neighbors forced the ashram to close. Locals were alarmed by the orange robes of the swami who performed fire rituals with Sri Ma, the sounds of God's name being chanted in a heathen tongue, and rumors of multi-armed deities inside the temple. The example of Jonestown was continually exhumed as an excuse to avoid accommodating a venerable but unfamiliar religion.

In a blue collar neighborhood in Martinez, California, across from a billowing oil refinery, Sri Ma and the Goddess idols she crafted herself finally found sanctuary. From 1987 till 1993, when the temple moved to a larger and more isolated plot in Napa County, she performed the *Chandi* daily and celebrated the frequent Hindu holidays.

Unlike most other spiritual adepts from India, Sri Ma did not advertise. Very few Americans interested in yoga, even those nearby in California, knew that a master of her caliber lived here. It was not Sri Ma's way to seek out disciples; trusting the ancient Vedic tradition, she knew that her disciples' own spiritual yearning would guide them to her. The fellowship that eventually found its way to the Mandir was, and still is, about half Indian; the other half, many of whom are Christians or Jews who had trained in meditation at other yoga institutions, came regularly to bask in Ma's presence. "It's one thing to read about saints," Dick Meigs, a Silicon Valley financier, told me. "It's another to live in the presence of one. Mother is always here for her children. I've learned so much just being with her. She doesn't teach; she doesn't have to. Just watching how she lives her life is the teaching. I have a wonderful mother, but Sri Ma has done more for me than my own mother ever did or ever could. She's a walking miracle."

Sri Ma's lifestyle was simple: rise hours before dawn, perform *pujas* (religious rituals) before the Shiva *lingam* on her personal altar, offering flowers to the photo of Ramakrishna beside the *lingam*, and then cooking, sewing, cleaning, and talking quietly with the unending stream of visitors who walked in the door at all hours of the day and night. Sometimes she mercy sat quietly with her devotees, her stillness suffusing the temple and their hearts.

I was deeply impressed by Ma's stillness. It is almost as if she wasn't there. There was no ego for me to catch hold of, describe, fight with, or surrender to. She was like a shadow, trailing silence. When she mentioned she would be returning to India and invited me to join her there, I knew instantly I would go.

§

Sri Ma grew up in Assam, one of India's northeasternmost provices, bordering Tibet, Burma, and Bhutan. Assam is home to Kamakhya, the holiest Goddess shrine in India, reputedly the ancient site of the Goddess' *yoni*. Ma will not be visiting Assam due to current political upheavals, so numbers of her Assamese devotees have made their way to the Mira Bai Mandir in Calcutta, where she is staying. From them we hear stories of Sri Ma's early days.

The story of Ma's life begins before her birth, during her mother's visit to the temple at Kamakhya. She was stopped by a *sadhu*, a wandering ascetic, who told her, "Come inside, I must initiate you in a special mantra. A very pure soul is coming to your family and you will have to be prepared. After she is born, bring her to me."

Sri Ma smiles as Mahavir relates the tale. "My mother took me to this *sadhu* when I was two months old. He whispered a mantra in my ear. I don't remember his face."

"Everyone knew there was something different about her, even when she was a child," Swami Satyananda adds. "When she was four years old, she was out in a fishing boat during a bad storm. The fishermen were panicking, till they noticed Sri Ma sitting calmly behind them. Her serenity calmed them down, and then the sea and the sky calmed down too. Ever after that, whenever the fisherman would see Sri Ma walking by the shore, they would pull their boats up onto the beach, run over and throw themselves down at her feet."

Often when villagers wanted to conduct a *puja* they would consult Ma, even though she had no formal religious training. She seemed to spontaneously know exactly how to perform the rites. They were also impressed by her inordinate devotion to Ramakrishna Paramahansa, who had worked as a priest in the Kali temple at Dakshineshwar, and whom she often saw in visions. The local people marvelled at the young girl's purity of character, cheerful servicefulness, and depth of wisdom. "A yogi wandering through our village warned her parents, 'Keep this girl close to you or you will lose her,'" a disciple relates. He was right; soon she disappeared.

For eight years Ma wandered through the jungles of Assam, only dimly in contact with external reality. "My devotees can tell you what happened then, that they saw me on this road, by that tree. I don't remember anything. I was 'crazy,' I went 'beyond' all the time."

"She was always in *samadhi*, the highest state of consciousness," says Mahavir. "It was difficult for us to bring her back to this world."

"Ma weighed about sixty pounds at that time, living on tulsi leaves and sandal water alone. She has gained so much weight!" Mahavir marvels as he looks at his guru for the first time in eight years. He lives directly behind the Kamakhya temple and used to see Ma often during her residence there. "You have been spoiling her in America!" he grins. She weighs ninety-seven pounds now.

I can't help reflecting that if Sri Ma had grown up in the United States, she would have been bundled off to a psychiatrist before she reached her teens, and probably would have spent most of her life on psychotropic medication. By Western standards, Sri Ma's state while she wandered in the jungles was obviously psychotic. But the psychotics I have met live fearful, fragmented lives, victims of visions that seal them off from the rest of humanity. Yet Sri Ma's centeredness, her connectedness, is extraordinary. She seems not abnormal but beyond normal, apparently dwelling in a state of consciousness that anger, desire and fear cannot penetrate.

§

"Let's go to Dakshineshwar!" Swami Satyananda suggests. It was at this famous temple that he first met Sri Ma twelve years ago. Ma agrees; taxis are hired and our group crowds into the cars for a chaotic ride through the Calcutta night to Bengal's most famous temple, the shrine to Goddess Kali, the Terrible Mother. It was here that Ramakrishna offered flowers and incense, rice and sweets to the idol of Kali until she came alive, lept off the pedestal and destroyed everything in him that was less than divine.

We arrive just as *arati*, the ceremonial waving of lights before the deity, concludes. I am struggling to catch a glimpse of the famous idol above the heads of the throngs gathered for vespers, when a devotee signals Swami Satyananda to come forward. As the doors to the deity's inner sanctum close to the public, the swami is ushered in and, shamelessly, I race up the stairs and slip through the door behind him. I am face to face with Kali.

Black as pitch, she wields bloodied weapons in each of her four hands. Her skirt is threaded with hacked limbs, her garland studded with decapitated human heads. She is stamping on a corpse. This is Ramakrishna's beloved deity, the Mother of the Universe. My mouth drops open, not because she is horrible but because she is beautiful. The Hindus have always understood this terrible beauty, the aspect of God that defies our reason and mocks our best intentioned plans, the part of God that is unmanageable.

Quietly Swami Satyananda begins to chant from the *Chandi, "Yah Devi sarva bhuteshu. . ."* ("I bow to the radiant Goddess who is consciousness itself, who appears in the form of bliss, peace, perfection, and death. To the Mother of all beings, again and again I bow!")

A brahmin fills our hands with flowers and escorts us out of the temple. Outside, Sri Ma's devotees are milling anxiously; *arati* is already over and Sri Ma has not yet appeared. Satyananda leads us across the courtyard to the Shiva temples that line the bank of the Ganges; we circumambulate each one.

I glance back at the deserted courtyard and in the dim light glimpse a pale apparition gliding rapidly over the cobblestone. My heart stops; I think I see Sarada Devi, Ramakrishna's wife, rushing to his room with a dish of his favorite foods, purees and fried eggplant.

Sarada Devi has accompanied us everywhere in Bengal. She peers down at us from grocery walls, her face is painted on the sides of trucks, her photo appears even on the dashboards of the taxis we have ridden. I doubt she ever imagined as she was growing up, a shy, illiterate peasant girl from the tiny village of Jayrambati, that before her death she would become a Goddess, the spiritual mother of Bengal.

When she was five years old, Sarada's parents betrothed her to a priest of the Dakshineshwar temple. He came to visit several times when she was a child; he seemed kind. But as the years passed and Sarada matured into womanhood, her husband-to-be did not reappear to claim his bride. Neighbors began to gossip; they said that the priest had gone mad, that Sarada might as well be widowed.

In her eighteenth year Sarada could bear to wait no longer, and with assertiveness uncharacteristic of her, asked her father to take her to Dakshineshwar to visit her finacè. There she discovered that Ramakrishna was not at all insane, but completely consumed by devotion to Mother Kali. Other temple priests were irritated with his unorthodox manners, but Rani Ma, the matron of the temple complex, was moved by his intense devotion and refused to fire him. Ramakrishna was not, and evidently never had been, interested in marriage, and probably had selected such a young bride to buy time for his continued spiritual practice, free from the burdens of marital responsibilities. Now his would-be wife was at his door and familial pressure to consummate the marriage ran high. "Will you drag me down into worldly life?" he demanded.

"No," Sarada responded. He married her.

In the meantime Bhairavi Ma, a highly accomplished tantric yogini, had taken an interest in Ramakrishna. Noting the fervor of his devotion, she took it upon herself to train him in the intricacies of yoga. He surpassed her every expectation; in fact, his skill in yoga was so awesome it almost frightened her. Techniques it had taken her a lifetime to learn he mastered in days. The scriptures state that a yogi could not sit in *samadhi* for more than 28 days without losing his body; Ramakrishna sat, unmoving, in the highest states of meditation for six continuous months. Devotees would force food into his mouth to prevent him from starving. Bhairavi knew that according to scripture, only God himself was capable of remaining in such elevated states for so long, and surviving. Her claims that her student was a divine incarnation met with incredulity from even Ramakrishna's most sympathetic admirers, but when she invited several of India's leading religious authorities to research the matter for themselves, and they ended their investigation prostrate at his feet, the laughing stopped. Sarada Devi discovered that she was married to God.

As Ramakrishna's fame grew and more and more devotees gathered around him (some of whom would eventually take their own place as giants in Indian history), Sarada remained in the background, serving her husband quietly with complete one pointedness. She was shocked when one day, full of divine spirit, Ramakrishna performed a *puja* to her, worshipping her as the Goddess herself.

It was after Ramakrishna's death that the cult of Sarada Devi began to grow. Ramakrishna had insisted that she must initiate disciples after his passing, a job that at first she lacked the confidence to do. Devotees, recalling that Ramakrishna had considered his wife a living embodiment of the Goddess, insisted that she take up the role of spiritual guide. And so ultimately, like Ramakrishna, Sarada initiated aspirants though, unlike her husband who would initiate only a select few specially trained students, she offered the mantra to everyone who came to her. Embodying the mother principle of the universe, she was incapable of turning anyone away.

Agonizingly shy from infancy, Sarada hid most of her adult life behind a veil. Devotees who came to Dakshineswar hoping for a glimpse of the Holy Mother might never see her in the temple. It was only after they left that they learned it was Sarada Devi who had swept their rooms and washed their bedsheets while they were meditating. Tales of her sanctity quickly spread throughout India. Wife of one of the greatest saints of the nineteenth century, Sarada matured into one of the greatest saints of the twentieth.

Traditionally Indian widows wear white saris. Sarada broke with this custom and wore her white sari with a distinctive red border. The figure slipping toward us across the empty courtyard is dressed in a white, red bordered sari. It is Sri Ma. My heart begins to beat again.

" I will take you to meet my son," Sri Ma announces.

Bob blanches and stutters, "Ma, I didn't realize—." Sri Ma only laughs and leads us Western pilgrims through the darkness to the Rama temple just outside Dakshineshwar. We approach the priests' living quarters and Ma begins to call, "Vashishta! Vashishta!"

A man at least twice Ma's age comes running out and lunges at Ma's feet. We Americans stand back in awe. This is the first true *sadhu* we have met in India. No one needs to tell us he is a *sadhu*—the light that emanates from him speaks for itself. He has what the Hindus call *tejas*—the unmistakable luminosity that comes from a life lived close to God. Vashishta, we learn, is the chief priest of this temple and a devotee of Sri Ma and Ramakrishna. He and Ma speak eagerly in Bengali, and then he turns to tell us, in heavily accented English, "You don't know how fortunate you are to be with this woman. You don't know what she is."

When we leave the temple we discover that one of the taxi drivers has absconded, taking with him Ma's sandals, which she left in the car. The Americans grumble but I secretly suspect that Bhumesvari, the Goddess of the earth, is praising the divine thief. Thanks to his cunning she continues to enjoy the bare-soled touch of the Mother's feet.

§

We are visiting Jayrambati, the birthplace of Sarada Devi. It began somewhat inauspiciously. As we got off the bus Ma had been leading us in devotional song when a monk from the

Ramakrishna order came rushing up shouting, "No singing! No singing! Please respect the sanctity of this place!"

Swami Satyananda joined in the monk's remonstrations, shouting at us in mock anger, "No singing! No prayer! Worship is not allowed in this temple!" The monk completely missed the irony in his tone.

In this village, however, we receive a warm welcome from Ganapati Mukerji, the nephew of Sarada Devi. Sri Ma had appeared somewhat disappointed with the house in which Sarada was raised which is now maintained by the Ramakrishna order. "It's different. They have changed it." But the hospitality of Sarada's family is overwhelming. Ganapati shows us the altar items with which he used to worship Sri Ma when her wandering brought her here years ago. "Please stay here," he pleads with her. "I will give you land. You can build an ashram."

Ma will be offered land at virtually every stop on our tour. "Everyone tells me, make temple here, make temple there," Ma responds. "I say no, make yourself. Make yourself! When flower is blossoming, bee will come."

Ganapati is offering sweets and our band of pilgrims is enjoying his stories about Sri Ma's early days in India. But I have to go to the bathroom. Now. That humorless malady the Indians wryly call "Delhi belly" has turned my gut to mulch. Purnima takes me by the arm out into the circuitous lanes to find the village latrine. I am impressed that she helps me so cheerfully when I am certain she would much rather be with Ma during this special time with Sarada Devi's family.

Purnima, I learn much later, was once an actress, a sophisticated woman of the world. When she first learned of Sri Ma, she went to her hoping for the saint's blessing. Ma refused to see her. She returned again and again; each time Ma had her devotees lock the door. For three years Ma would not allow Purnima into her presence.

Finally one day while Purnima was away, Sri Ma went to her home. The servants let her in and Ma spent hours cleaning the house and setting up an altar for worship and meditation. When Purnima returned she was stunned. Who had done this astonishing thing? "Sri Ma," her servants replied. Weeping with joy and sorrow, Purnima ran to Ma's ashram.

The door was locked.

Purnima spent weeks sitting before the new altar in her home, crying and calling out to Ma. On a still, full moon night, Purnima once again walked to Sri Ma's ashram. The door opened and Purnima stepped into the everlasting embrace of the Mother of the Universe.

§

There is no end to Calcutta. It sprawls around us everywhere, so heavily polluted by fumes of diesel fuel and burning cow dung that we find ourselves coughing like veteran smokers. There are cows everywhere, perfect embodiments of faith and serenity as they lie in the midst of the streets while anarchic traffic careens around them.

"It's beautiful. Everything is beautiful," Sri Ma is saying, here in the ugliest city in the world. "God is everywhere. He is in the forest, he is in the villages, he is here. You cannot say he is not here."

Ma is leading us through the back alleys of Calcutta to visit her poorest devotees. This is a day they will cherish for their entire lives: the day the Mother stepped into their home. "She stood here," they will tell their grandchildren. "She sat there. She chanted *Govinda Krishna Jai.*"

I am horrified when Manju will not allow me to enter her house until she has personally bathed my feet. Tears are streaming down her cheeks as she tenderly wipes away the soil of India. "In India," the swami explains, "it's considered a great blessing to wash the feet of the devotees."

"Then I should be washing hers," I protest.

As in most of the homes we visit in India, the walls are covered with pictures of saints and deities. There is Ramakrishna, Vivekananda, Lokanath. And there is the Goddess Durga, plunging her trident through the buffalo demon Mahisha.

As the devotees chatter, I learn that an elderly Indian woman who slept in the same room with me the previous night was Sri Ma's mother, visiting from Assam. I would never have guessed there was a connection—Sri Ma had not behaved toward her in any special manner I could detect. Then it occurs to me that it was not so much that Sri Ma treated her mother like the rest of us, as that she treats everyone she meets with as much respect and attention as she does her own mother.

We move on to Malati's home. Malati is one of Sri Ma's richest Calcutta devotees. When our group of pilgrims first arrived in Calcutta, only to learn that our luggage had somehow made its way to Bangladesh, it was Malati who rushed out to buy us all a change of clothes. Her wealth is obvious the moment we step into the house. There is a telephone. There is a toilet. Malati proudly displays the piece de la resistance: a black and white television set. She offers to turn it on for us; we demur.

We are ushered into Malati's bedroom and all of us are seated on her bed; high, stiff beds double as couches almost everywhere in India. On Malati's altar there is the usual portrait of Sarada Devi, but some artist has adroitly superimposed Sri Ma's features over Sarada's. It is very striking.

Malati invites us to the Bipatarini Chandi Mandir, a temple she helped finance in Rajpur, outside Calcutta. There is no use protesting; cars are hired and we are bundled off on yet another bumpy, noisy ride through this city of twelve million. Finally the shacks and dust covered, open air shops slip away and we roar into village India.

As we step onto the Bipatarini ashram grounds, Johnathan and I look at each other, eyes round with wonder. "This is *Svarga,* heaven!" we exclaim simultaneously. Peace lies over the grounds like a baby's soft cotton blanket. Shady trees freely offer coconuts, bananas, mangoes, and jack fruit. In large, shallow ponds villagers cheerfully wash their clothes. Ashram residents appear, delighted to see us, to show us the facilities, to answer our questions, to feed us. Their faces are radiant with joy. I have visted many ashrams in the United States but have never experienced one like this, where everyone is full of happiness and the spirit of selfless service. "This is a real ashram," Sri Ma concurs. "We stay here and do *tapasya.*"

Who is the guru here? we want to know. Their late teacher Baba Dulal, we are told, did *tapasya* here for many years, fasting and worshiping and meditating, and by the tree now decorated with a red ribbon he was finally blessed with a vision of the Divine Mother. The tree is marked by a *bedi,* a sort of concrete ring which protects it and also serves as a seat for meditators. The sense of sanctity around the tree is remarkable. I can feel the continuing force of Baba Dulal's meditation.

Just before he died, we learn later, Baba Dulal predicted that within two years Westerners would come to this ashram to worship. It had been almost exactly two years since his death when we walked in the gate.

Swami and Ma are already seated in a clearing near the *bedi* chanting the *Chandi.* Several of the Westerners chant the shorter *Devi Gita,* The Song of the Goddess. I close my eyes in meditation. I feel like I am floating in the sky. Two hours flash by in the space of a breath. ·

The residents take us to see their *murtis,* the statues of saints and Gods before which they worship. Many of the saints depicted here are Goddess worshipers: Ramakrishna, Adi Shankaracharya, Ramprasad Sen, Lahiri Mahasaya. There are statues of Lakshmi, the smiling Goddess of good fortune, and of Vishnu, the hero of the universe who manifested on earth five thousand years ago as the Yadava prince Krishna (speaker of the *Bhagavad Gita*), and thousands of years earlier still as Rama, the ideal husband and king. They want to show us one more statue, the one Baba Dulal himself designed, depicting the vision he had seen under the tree. We are brought before the final *murti* and my knees almost give way.

There, towering above us, is a twenty foot tall Durga, one foot resting on a huge lion, the other pinning down the screaming demon king, Mahisha, as she runs her trident through his heart. Painted on the wall around the statue are Gods hailing her victory, and the host of demons, looking on in terror as Mahisha is destroyed. "My God!" Cathy exclaims. The rest of us can scarcely speak. The *murti* is so lifelike that Cathy swears afterwards she saw the Goddess' eyes move.

Standing beneath her we all glimpse the universal process that she is, how inexorably she will crush us all—annihilating the Mahishas within every one of us—obliterating everything that is less than herself. This is the Universal Mother and here is her merciless grace. "Please don't invoke Kali," a poet wrote, "if you want to live as you've lived before."

Sri Ma slips behind the screen separating us from the *murti* and, climbing onto it, reaches up to touch Durga's raised foot.

§

The patrons of the Mira Bai Mandir, owners of a chain of American restaurants called Gaylords, have invited Swami Satyananda and Ma to lead a *satsang* in the temple this evening. Swami will give a little talk and "Sri Ma's Dog and Pony Show," as we Western pilgrims have dubbed ourselves, will lead the *kirtan*, the religious singing. Afterward devotees can come forward for Mother's personal blessing.

The temple is packed; hundreds of devotees are sitting on the floor beneath the temple deities: Parvati and her consort, Lord Shiva; Sita and her husband, Rama; Radha and her lover, Krishna. Our group launches into one of my favorite *bhajans* by the great poet Ramprasad:

> One day the time will come,
> one day the time will come

when I call Tara! Tara! Tara!
and tears will fall from my eyes.

From the bottom of our hearts we call out to Tara—the Goddess who carries her children safely across the roiling sea of life to that Other Shore. Suddenly my eyes are wet.

Our songs end and instantly the crowd is surging forward, each devotee hoping to receive some words of comfort or advice from the Holy Mother, a promise that a child will be born, a prophecy of financial relief, healing for a disease. There are hundreds of them.

Sri Ma flees.

Saints of every personality type have graced the shores of India. There have been nonviolent saints and irascible saints, intellectual saints and ecstatic saints, warrior saints and renunciates. Some have lived in palaces, others have made themselves at home on piles of dung. Some saints walk among the masses; others, like Sri Ma, are deeply private individuals who would like nothing better than to sit alone in a small temple, doing *puja* and offering prayers. The many long days visiting devotee after devotee have been a strain on her, much as she loves these people. But for her delicate nature, this horde is too much.

How does a yogini flee? Ma raises her right hand in blessing, closes her eyes, and merges into God. Her breath stops; her body does not move at all. She is in *samadhi,* the state of divine union. The waves of peace emanating from that tiny body engulf everyone in the temple.

The atmosphere in the hall completely changes. One moment it is a circus, barely under control. The next, silent awe sweeps over the crowd and quietly, one by one, they move forward to touch the feet of the Mother. They received a far greater blessing than they had anticipated this night.

On her flight to the divine, Sri Ma has carried every heart in this room with her.

§

We are somewhere in rural Bengal when our small jeep gives up the ghost. We fourteen pilgrims, some of whom have been sitting in each other's laps, some with our legs dangling out the windows, scramble out into the Indian dusk. Our breakdown provides the local evening entertainment; the entire village turns out to stare. Undoubtedly there are younger faces among those here who have never seen a white person before; Sri Ma has definitely not been leading us on well beaten tourist trails. Swami Satyananda trots off to find a telephone; miraculously there is one at a small shop nearby.

An hour and a half later (please understand that by Indian standards this means instantaneously) police jeeps swoop down upon us, and we are carried off to the home of our rescuer, Sultan Singh, Inspector General of the West Bengal police and a longtime devotee of Ma's. There is nothing he is not willing to do for us. Essentially he places the facilities, vehicles, and personnel of the Bengal police department at Sri Ma's disposal. I am initially shocked at this casual manipulation of public resources for private benefit, until I remember that this is a country where saints are valued as much as Americans venerate movie stars and professional athletes. Singh is treating Ma as a very distinguished visiting dignitary.

Singh's home is beyond belief. Built by the Portuguese two hundred years before my country was founded, it is constructed so solidly I believe it could withstand a direct nuclear attack. Each room is about four times the size of my apartment, and there are many, many rooms. The ceilings are 20 feet high. Relaxing on the verandah overlooking the Ganges, Sri Ma suddenly remarks how much this house reminds her of her childhood home. Inspired by the gurgling of the sacred river only yards beyond the veranda, Swami Satyananda begins to speak on the spiritual reality behind this *maya*.

In Hindu Tantra, the static, unchanging reality is referred to as male, while the active, dynamic aspect is called female, the *shakti*. In Sri Ma and Satyananda's case, the gender roles seem reversed. Sri Ma is usually silent. When someone brings a question about God or spiritual life, she quietly signals the Swami, and with great delight he expounds for hours. He is her *shakti*. She remains in the reality; he articulates her experience. It is a fascinating symbiosis.

Sultan Singh turns to Ma. "You look like Sarada Devi," he says pointedly.

She ignores him and, suddenly uncharacteristically talkative, begins chatting with the women in Bengali.

§

We are barrelling down the national highway in a donated school bus at thirty-five miles per hour. This speed feels reckless as we bounce through the gaping potholes that everywhere pock the road. The traffic is chaotic beyond imagination; enormous, brightly painted trucks ("goods carriages") plunge headlong at each other, missing each other by a fraction of an inch, and sometimes not missing each other at all. Three-wheeled autorickshaws run bicycles off the road; tank-like automobiles run autorickshaws off the road; trucks run cars off the road.

We see a five year old boy lying in the street, his brain splattered for yards along the pavement, today's fresh road kill in a country that cannot be bothered with traffic laws, where motorized vehicles are a means of population control.

"He is dead," Ma says quietly. "This is his *karma*. We have to accept."

I sit back in my seat. It will take me some time to digest this. But the Mother of the Universe has already assimilated the dead child back into her own ravenous being.

§

I am thrilled with Benares. Billed as the oldest continuously inhabited city in the world (this city was ancient six thousand years ago, when the Vedas were composed), I had imagined it would be filthy and decrepit. Instead I discover one of the most staggeringly beautiful cities in the world. Cars cannot penetrate the tiny lanes of the Old City; as we approach the ashram where we will be staying we are obliged to clamber out of our taxis, throw our luggage over our backs, and walk.

Sri Ma has stayed at the Trailinga Swami Ashram before. The ashram manager is waiting for us by the door, eager for a glimpse of Ma.

We leave our luggage in our room on the roof, ducking the playful monkeys who leap from rooftop to rooftop, and stopping to pet the calf that lives on top of the building. Then we see something completely unprecedented: Sri Ma is excited. We follow her down the broad steps of Panchaganga Ghat (the very spot where the Muslim poet sage Kabir tricked the Hindu guru Ramananda into initiating him in the Ram mantra five centuries ago!) and, squealing with delight, Ma throws herself into the Ganges. She immerses herself again and again in the holy river reputed to wash away sin. "This is for Parvati! This is for Gotam! This is for Jit!" she calls out the names of her devotees who have remained in America as she offers handfuls of sacred water back to the river.

Ma wants to bring our group of ten American pilgrims to Vishvanath, one of the three most sacred temples of Hinduism. Along with an entourage of enthusiastic Indian devotees, we clambor into a small wooden boat and a teenager rows us half the length of the city of Benares to the Vishvanath dock. I am feeling terrible about how hard the poor boy is slaving to row the overloaded boat this far, and all for forty rupees (hardly more than a dollar), till I notice that twenty minutes later he has not broken a sweat; he is not even breathing hard. My God, I think, our cardiovascular researchers should examine this heart! Ma leads the group in robust song as we float past the breathtaking ghats, *"Jai Ma, jai Ma/Jai jai Ma!"* (Victory to the Divine Mother! Victory! Victory!) All along the bank people look up from their laundry and bathing to watch the crazy Americans glide past, glorifying the Goddess.

As we approach Vishvanath, the words from an Indian *bhajan* I have sung a hundred times play through my mind, *"Hara Hara Mahadeva Shambho/Kashi Vishvanatha Gange!"* (Hail to the great God Shiva, who dwells at the Vishvanth temple in Benares near the bank of the Ganges!) Sri Ma guides our group toward the inner sanctum where the most sacred of India's *lingams* is kept. Abruptly furious brahmins appear shouting, "Non-Hindus not allowed!" Bob steps back in shock; Marianne begins to cry. We try to explain that some of us have been practicing aspects of the Hindu faith for twenty years but the brahmins will not listen. An orange-robed renunciate appears, looking horribly distressed, and calls out, "No, no, no! Vishvanath is for all! Please come in!" but our way remains barred. The scene grows increasingly tense as angry priests crowd the small temple.

Finally Sri Ma leads us out onto the narrow street. Standing serenely outside the temple, Ma announces as calmly as if she were noting the time of day, "Mother has never placed a curse. Today I place a curse. The brahmins will be destroyed. Mother will be established in the temple."

We follow Sri Ma to the Ganges. She steps into the water, saying, "Mother Ganga accepts everyone. She will never turn anyone away." Cupping the holy water in her hands, Ma asks us to pray with her, "We are all one. May everyone see that we are all one. May there be no hatred anywhere." I wade out into the clear, bright river, offering my handful of water back to the Ganges, and watch as the drops merge seamlessly into the stream.

§

Unknown to us, the incident at Vishvanath has caused a furor in Benares. The fact that Ma had cursed the temple has seriously shaken a lot of people: in India curses of the God-realized souls are not taken lightly. Evidently, the temple brahmins were swamped with protests.

A week later we receive a phone call from the Vishvanath priests. Our group is welcome in the temple at any time, and the policy regarding the barring of non-Hindus is being reconsidered.

I understand now that the Mother's curse is her left-handed blessing; like a mother gently swatting a child on its bottom, it is her way of moving us along.

§

"Ma," I ask late one night, as we settle onto the couch at Mira Bai Mandir, "Sarada Devi told Ramakrishna she was completely disgusted with human life and that she would not return to this planet under any circumstances. He scolded her and told her she would have to come back to serve the devotees. Then he promised that he himself would return in a hundred years. Ma, it's been a hundred years now. Is he here?"

"He is here," she quietly replies. "Open your spiritual eye. You will see."

§

Though I have learned a great deal from Sri Ma, there is still one issue about which I am profoundly uncomfortable. The vestiges of my Christian upbringing make me feel that calling anyone, no matter how saintly, a God or a Goddess is, well, blasphemous. "I call Sri Ma the Divine Mother because, like Ramakrishna and Jesus and Moses and other great beings, she has merged her consciousness completely in the divine," Swami Satyananda responds. "In India, when we see a saint who is merged in the Supreme Reality, we say that even though they appear to be limited beings like us, their essence is one with God, and therefore they are God. The truth is that we're all incarnations of God, it's just that the saints know they are."

But no skeptical questions can dampen Swami's mood today. He has just received an answer from the priests at Dakshineshwar in response to Sri Ma's request that she be allowed to perform a special twenty-four hour *puja* to the Goddess at the temple. For the first time in over one hundred years, the brahmins have given permission to conduct this rite. The last time this *puja* was done it was performed by Ramakrishna himself. If Ma is happy with the news, her face does not betray it. Instead the Mother of the Universe sits down by a basket of flowers and serenely begins preparing garlands.

Anandamayi Ma: The Bliss-Permeated Mother

*L*aughing and joking, Bholanath Chakravarti was bringing home a friend to show off his pretty wife. When they burst in the door however, Bholanath's wife didn't move but continued sitting silently on the floor with a shawl draped over her head. Annoyed that she didn't leap up to greet them, Bholanath snapped, "Can't you see you have a guest? Who do you think you are?"

Slowly the young woman lifted the cloth from her face. The energy emanating from her was so intense that, as they recalled later, both men involuntarily leapt backward. *"Purna brahma narayana,"* she replied. "I am the all pervading reality." One of the most extraordinary sages of modern times had just unveiled herself.

Nirmala Sundari (Sanskrit for "Immaculate Beauty," an apt name for a woman whose physical and spiritual beauty were both breathtaking) was born in 1896 in Kheora, East Bengal (modern Bangladesh). By the time of her death in 1982, this virtually illiterate village girl would be revered throughout the world as Anandamayi Ma, the Bliss-Permeated Mother.

Nirmala was remembered by neighbors and relations as an exceptionally cheerful and luminous—but not particularly intelligent—child. Her tendency to abruptly stop all activity and stare abstractedly into space for long periods made her parents uneasy. Their concern had begun at the very moment of her birth when the newborn infant did not cry. Years later when her mother recalled this alarming event, Nirmala responded, "Why should I have cried? I was watching the trees through the slats in the window."

Nirmala enjoyed barely two years of education before being drafted out of school to begin full-time housekeeping. Her parents arranged her betrothal to Bholanath in 1909; she moved in with him five years later. Bholanath must have considered himself the luckiest man on earth when he saw his stunning bride. He was blessed indeed, but not in the manner he'd hoped for; his wife flatly refused to have sex with him. His consternation turned to horror when he awoke in the night to find Nirmala curling her body into contorted shapes on the floor and making odd, nonsensical sounds. He became convinced she was possessed and actually consulted an exorcist. Neither Bholanath nor Nirmala had formal religious training, so neither recognized at the time that Nirmala was spontaneously assuming hatha yoga postures or that her strange vocalizations were in fact sacred mantras.

From 1918 through 1924, Nirmala disinterestedly watched herself passing through the various stages of *sadhana,* spiritual practice. From the moment of her fully conscious birth, as she lay watching the trees, Nirmala apparently remained in the state of *sakshin,* as the lucid witnessing state is called in yoga. She did not perceive herself to be doing anything. It was all just happening. "What I am I have always been, even from my infancy," she later reported. "Nevertheless, different stages of *sadhana* manifested through this body. Wisdom was revealed in a piecemeal fashion, integral knowledge was broken into parts." Nirmala—born experiencing the unity of all creation—found it astonishing to experience the world in bits and pieces, as the rest of us do.

Nirmala's unorthodox behavior shocked her family many times throughout her life. One such occasion occurred when she refused to bow down to her elders, a societal nicety considered *de rigeuer* in Bengal. But Nirmala had heard a voice telling her, "You are not to bow down to anyone. Whom do you want to make obeisance to? You are everything."

"At once," Nirmala states, "I realized that the universe was all my own manifestation. Partial knowledge gave way to the universal and I found myself face to face with the One that appears as the many." This—the culmination of all mystical endeavor— would be quite an achievement for anyone, much less for a young woman who had never had a guru.

It wasn't that the issue of a guru, or spiritual guide, hadn't come up. Friends who knew of Nirmala's otherworldly inclinations strongly encouraged her to seek out a teacher to formally initiate

her into spiritual life. She went to the local pandits but no one was interested in teaching a poor, illiterate village girl. On August 3, 1922, in a total break with the entire history of Hindu religious tradition, Nirmala Sundari Chakravarti sat down and initiated herself. Yoga teaches that the guru, the mantra he or she imparts during initiation, and the disciple are in reality, one. Already established in that indivisible reality, Anandamayi Ma dramatized this unity when she played the parts of teacher and student stimultaneously, her higher Self conferring the mantra on the lower self. Thus she received a mantra directly from the divinity within and went on to become one of the few sages of Hinduism who, like Brahmajna Ma (Mother of Supreme Knowledge) and Ramana Maharshi, achieved total enlightenment without the aid of a guru.

By 1922 Nirmala's bewildered husband Bholanath had seen enough to realize that his wife was not possessed by demons. If anything, he concluded, she was possessed by God. He became her first disciple—a gesture that scandalized many Indians. Till the day Anandamayi Ma died, the ultra-orthodox maintained it was not proper for a male to bow at his own wife's feet.

In 1924 Bholanath got his lucky break—he was offered a job as superintendent of Shahbag Gardens in Dhakka. He and Nirmala moved into a cottage on the Shahbag estate and while Bholanath tended the grounds, Nirmala tended a growing number of devotees. Rumors of miraculous healings drew some, others came for the music; Nirmala's voice, as she chanted the glories of God, was sublime. Mother of Shahbag the locals began to call her, though it would not be long before they called her the Mother of the World.

The words of this radiant woman amazed her visitors. She spoke of states beyond time and space with authority, as if she knew them intimately. "Time devours ceaselessly. No sooner is childhood over than youth takes its place—the one swallows up the other. This occurs so slowly that one hardly notices it happening. But in reality, appearance, continuance, and disappearance occur simultaneously in one place. Everything is infinite; infinity and finitude are indeed the same. There is one thread in a garland, yet there are gaps between the flowers. It is the gaps that cause want and sorrow. To fill them is to be free." Nirmala taught her rapt students to fill in the gaps with love for God and surrender to His will. But God, she insisted, was not only the creator of the universe but also the essence of one's own being. "Man's true nature—call it what you will—is the supreme Self of all."

In 1924 Nirmala stopped feeding herself. She noted with characteristic dispassion that her hands simply would not carry food to her mouth. For the rest of her life, her devotees had to feed her like a young child.

At midnight on June 2, 1932, Nirmala called together a handful of close disciples and made a startling announcement. She was leaving. Why? her devotees pleaded. Where would she go? She didn't know, she explained, and left immediately. She settled for a year in a deserted Shiva temple near Dehradun, apparently undergoing severe penance but in fact, by her own admission, remaining in unutterable bliss. For Bholanath, who remained in the dilapidated hovel with her, the experience may have been somewhat less than delightful. At any rate, this was the last site at which Anandamayi Ma can be said to have lived; after this she moved constantly, ashrams and charitable institutions springing up everywhere she paused.

Nirmala was by no means without spiritual guidance, the lack of an external guru notwithstanding. Her *kheyal,* or Inner Guide, directed her life course—sometimes, from the point of view of her devotees, rather erratically. The hundreds of stories about Anandamayi Ma's *kheyal* are legendary. For example, one evening in the midst of a *kirtan* (religious songfest), Nirmala stood up and walked rapidly out of the house. Two devotees ran after, asking where she was headed. "Sarnath," she replied.

Sarnath was many miles away. "Why are you going tonight?" the devotees wanted to know. "There isn't any train to Sarnath at this hour!" Nirmala continued at a brisk pace to the train station. At her request, one devotee bought a ticket for the mail train which would pass near Sarnath but was not scheduled to stop there. Outside Sarnath, the train inexplicably stopped. Nirmala and her two befuddled devotees leapt off. "Which way to the Birla Hotel?" she demanded. They had no idea. She strode purposefully forth, her tiny entourage scurrying to keep up.

The hotel came into sight and the three pilgrims burst in. Nirmala ignored the host and headed directly for a guest room. As they approached, the devotees heard a woman in the room wailing. Nirmala pounded on the door calling, "It's all right! I'm here!" The door opened and the devotees were astonished to see Maharattan, a fellow disciple. Maharattan had been stranded penniless in Sarnath a few hours previously, and had been crying to Anandamayi Ma ever since.

Nirmala spent the rest of the evening teasing Maharattan about her fear. This experience undoubtedly cured the grateful devotee of any anxiety for some time to come!

When in 1955 the district magistrate of Vindhyachal learned that Anandamayi Ma was visiting his area, he rushed to have her *darshan* (the blessing of seeing a saint in person). Ma appeared to have been expecting him and took him out on the verandah. Pointing to the ground below she instructed, "Gods and Goddesses are lying under the earth here. They told me it is very irksome to remain buried there and they would like to be taken out. Can you help them?"

The magistrate immediately assembled a work crew and began to dig. It was tough work, cutting through solid rock. By the second day the crew was completely disgusted, seriously questioning whether the magistrate had lost his mind. On the third day they uncovered 200 exquisite ancient idols buried in the dirt.

Anandamayi Ma was embraced not only by the simple people but by India's greatest scholars, saints, and politicians (including Mahatma Gandhi, who met her in 1942, and Indira Gandhi, an admirer of hers since childhood). When the greatest scholar of India, Gopinatha Kaviraj, visited Ma, the answers to his abstruse philosophical questions that this uneducated woman instantly offered so greatly astonished him that he moved into her ashram, where he spent the rest of his life.

The esteem in which Anandamayi Ma was held is reflected in the events surrounding her appearances at India's *kumbha melas,* religious fairs which draw millions of pilgrims, including the heads of many of India's leading religious institutions. The rivalry between the various religious leaders is well known and, unfortunately at times, flavors the *melas* with pettiness rather than with the spirit of harmony the fairs were intended to promote. In the last decade of Ma's life, there appeared to be only one thing the religious dignitaries at the *kumbha mela* could agree on: all went to Ma's tent to bow reverently before the aging woman whose sanctity was so fully evident that even the most rancorous left his egotism with his sandals outside the door. Feuding brahmins would appear asking Ma to arbitrate their disputes; after several minutes in her silent, luminous company, their arguments would fade and they would energe from the tent beaming and embracing. It was here that Ma was finally acknowledged as the Universal Mother, the saint whose compassion knew no boundaries of caste, creed, or nationality, the saint before whom all, regardless of their background, were awed into stillness.

Paramahansa Yogananda's meeting with Ma as chronicled in his classic *Autobiography of a Yogi* was for many Westerners their first introduction to Anandamayi Ma. Her reply to his request that she tell him about herself bears repeating: "My consciousness has never associated itself with the temporal body. Before I came to this earth I was the same. As a little girl I was the same. I grew into womanhood, but still I was the same. And in front of you now, I am the same. Ever afterwards though the dance of creation changes around me in the hall of eternity, I shall remain the same."

Many of the world's great spiritual traditions speak of an unchanging reality behind the flux of material life, a sort of being-ness that remains even after the universe itself dissolves. The goal of yoga is to subside back into this ground of being, the luminous clarity of Buddhism, the "Godhead behind God" of Christian mystic Meister Eckhart. Anandamayi Ma's words, and even more her life, reveal that she was continually immersed in the ocean of pure being that remains ever the same.

Anandamayi Ma did not write or lecture; she merely lived in the divine presence, moment to moment. From her point of view she did not serve others because she did not see others as separate from herself; to remove their pain was simply to relieve her own. Though her devotees watched her travel throughout India, she never went anywhere: "For this body the question of coming and going does not arise at all. This body neithers comes or goes anywhere. The whole universe is this body's home. Where can this body go? There is only one all-pervading consciousness everywhere. There is no space for the body to move or even turn around. Even if pushed away, it is still there," she explained.

Fortunately for posterity, several of Anandamayi Ma's followers wrote down her answers to their questions; these logs constitute the body of her message to humanity. Of worldly desires she said, "If you desire fame or wealth, God will give it to you, but you will not feel satisfied. The kingdom of consciousness is a unity, and until you experience it in its totality, you will never be content. God grants you a little bit of his joy at a time to keep your discontent alive, for without that discontent you will not progress. You, a child of immortality, can never feel at home in the realm of death, nor will God allow you to remain here. Remember that the heartache you experience is the beginning of an awakening in consciousness."

Why are there different religions, and so much conflict between them? "Controversy belongs to the path, but actually everyone is in his own home. The same path is not for everyone. Even within a family, each child has different inclinations. Spiritual seekers are each molded in a unique way, but each will have to pass through the gate of truth."

What is the guru? "Everybody is a guru. Every person from whom one has learned something, no matter how little, can be called one's guru. But the real guru is the one whose teaching guides you toward Self realization. Pray continually to God that he may reveal himself to you as your spiritual teacher. In reality, however, the guru dwells within, and unless you discover the inner guru, nothing can be achieved."

Ma described the experience of the mystic as a sort of drowning. "Suppose some people go to bathe in the sea. One whose only goal is the ocean itself will not look back to the shore. Give yourself up to the wave and you will be absorbed by the current; having dived into the sea, you do not return anymore. The eternal himself is the wave that floods the shore so that you may be carried away. If your aim is the supreme, you will be led on by the movement of your true nature. In the guise of the wave, he holds out his hand and calls to you, 'Come!'"

Anandamayi Ma taught that the only reality is divine reality; that our perception of ourselves as apart from God is only a dream, a superimposition of ignorance; and that those who release their hold on their petty desires and selfish motives, turning wholeheartedly to the divine not in heaven but in themselves, can live every moment in perfect bliss. Of this, she was herself a living example.

"Laugh as much as you can. By this all the rigid knots in your body will be loosened. Making the interests of others your own, seek refuge at his feet in total surrender. You will then see how the laughter that flows from your heart will lighten the world."

Anandamayi Ma's greatest contribution was not so much what she did or said; it is more what she was. She amazed and inspired millions—first in India, then throughout the world—by her pure being: unceasingly radiant, merged entirely in the divine, and yet constantly sensitive to the needs of all who came to her. States of perfection that yoga students read about in books were physically demonstrated by this woman who moved in divine awareness as effortlessly as others shift through the air.

Ma's enigmatic reply to her devotees' frequently-voiced question, "Who are you?" was "I am whatever you think me to be." Perhaps this was a clue that Anandamayi Ma was merely the mirror of that which is purest and most wondrous within ourselves, and that the purpose of her being was only to show us what we all can be.

To us today the semi-literate village girl from Bengal offers a radical example of a truly liberated woman, a human being who loved everyone who came to her as if they were her own children, and yet remained unattached to anyone; who served others constantly without concerning herself about whether they were appropriately grateful. Throughout her extensive travels she never displayed fear; she doesn't appear to have been capable of conceiving of any reality other than the bliss at the core of her own being. She perceived this bliss pervading all beings everywhere so what was there to be afraid of? According to Indian mystical literature, travelling pennilessly from one end of the Indian subcontinent to the other requires no more courage for a person in that state of awareness than strolling through a garden.

Carol Devi made three trips to India to walk with Ma in that garden. "She had such an amazing presence and amazing being. The power of her presence radiated to such a broad circumference. You didn't often get to be quiet because there were so many people around her, but you didn't even need to try to meditate. Her vibrations were so strong she thrust you into meditation.

"Ma supported you in whatever *sadhana* (spiritual practice) you had; that was your tradition. All beliefs and dogmas were all one under Ma. It didn't matter what religion you were. There was no feeling one religion was better than another." If you were a devoted Christian, for example, but wished to be initiated in meditation, Ma would give you Jesus' name as your mantra. And unlike some teachers, who forbid their devotees to pay homage to other saints, Anandamayi Ma didn't hesitate to allow Carol to visit other sages. Ma never stressed loyalty; "I could go to any group I wanted. But there was never any doubt in my mind who my guru was.

"I had a totally intimate relationship with Ma, but everyone in the room had the same experience. It was like Krishna with the *gopis.*" All the *gopis,* the village girls who tended the cows, were in love with the avatar Krishna as he grew up in rural Vrindavan. One night to satisfy their desires he invited them into the forest. Then he emanated from himself dozens of identical Krishnas, each dancing through the mystical night with a different *gopi.* Every girl believed she was alone with the Lord, that he belonged to her only. Just so Carol Devi was the most special person in the world to Ma. But so was every other soul who entered the saint's presence.

Even though Anandamayi Ma was already elderly when Carol first met her, keeping up with the aged saint was grueling. The constant travel and difficult conditions in South Asia left Carol exhausted. "Yet it was spiritually exhilarating. It was like walking with Jesus."

American born Hari Priya wrote Anandamayi Ma asking if she might be permitted to see her. Ma wrote back, "You're always welcome to visit me. If it is time for you to come, God will make the arrangements." Travel money materialized out of the ether and two weeks later Hari Priya was in Dehra Dun. She would make ten more trips to India to be with Ma, all together spending four years in her presence. "If Christ or any other holy person were on earth I would go to see them. So of course I went to Ma."

Hari Priya can hardly restrain her tears as she remembers her first sight of Ma. Ma walked into the room carrying a flower. "I started crying. I didn't have any Indian manners, I didn't know what to do like bowing, so I hugged her." In the Hindu culture of the time, for a stranger, especially an outcaste Westerner, to walk up and physically embrace an orthodox Indian was horrifyingly inappropriate. But the Mother understood. "She asked me my name and gave me the flower." Arrangements were made so that Hari Priya could live nearby. "That first trip was our honeymoon. I sat one foot away from her during her *darshans.*"

Subsequent trips were not always so easy. "A lot of times she ignored me. This was to break my ego. I had a lot of subtle spiritual pride. Ma was chopping at the root of it. Then she would fill me up again with her bliss by doing something special." Hari Priya remembers with special fondness the time Mother sat holding her hand and told her, "You came all this way for love of me. You've suffered so much for this body. That is your greatness."

"What do you want, the inner or the outer?" Ma asked Hari Priya on another occasion.

"I want it all!" Hari Priya exclaimed and explained, "She made every situation a spiritual power house, a heaven."

"For the most part Ma would sit quietly. She could also be jolly and tell wonderful stories. Her charm was all encompassing. She'd be telling a story and lean forward and whisper, and make it so intimate.

"I felt every word that came out of her mouth was God's name. It vibrated with spiritual power. And I didn't even know her language! She was totally God-centered all the time. Her laughter was transcendental—it would pierce your heart."

Hari Priya remembers the time one devotee mentioned to another that Ma rarely bathed. "She didn't need to, her body was so pure. It had a unique fragrance, like lotus, banana, and sandalwood." The day after the disciple made this remark Ma took thirty baths. The devotee reframed from making similar comments in the future.

Hari Priya remembers the terrible day in 1982, just nine days before she was to leave for her tenth trip to India, that a fellow disciple called. "She didn't have to say it. I knew it from the sound of her voice." Hari Priya put down the phone and began to sob. She returned to India anyway, visiting the ashrams in Pune, Hardwar, and Dehra Dun. "Her presence was still so strong. I'd weep because I couldn't see her. It was like having an invisible mother."

Anandamayi Ma had stepped into another part of the garden. Carol Devi sighs, "There's not a day that passes that I don't remember her. Ask any of Ma's devotees and they'll say the same thing. The tiger has you in her embrace!"

I stare up at the white mansion visible from our boat on the Ganges. Large Hindi letters proclaim that this is the Benares ashram of Anandamayi Ma. To my enormous regret, I have arrived far too late to meet one of the greatest saints of all time. It is now more than a decade since the physical body of Anandamayi Ma passed from this world (Ma herself, of course, would insist that she hasn't gone anywhere—that she remains, as ever, the same), but her legacy of love and wisdom will endure as long as humanity cherishes that small number of remarkable beings we call saints, those who point beyond the limitations of our ordinary awareness to a state of being as broad and blissful as the universe itself.

Anandi Ma: Awakening the Kundalini

*A*nandi Ma first met her guru, Dhyanyogi Madhusudandas, when she was fourteen, under most unusual circumstances. It was the last day of Nava Ratri, a ten day festival devoted to the Divine Mother, and the family priest asked Anandi Ma to repeat some mantras to the Goddess. As she uttered the words, Anandi Ma entered a state of meditation so profound that no one could rouse her. At one point she fell over; her head landed in the fire pit where the ritual was being conducted, but she was not burned. Her father, amazed and alarmed, hurried to Dhyanyogi hoping the sage would know how to restore the girl to her senses. An eyewitness reports that the moment he saw Anandi Ma, Dhyanyogi exclaimed, "This is the one I've been waiting for!" and gently guided her back to waking consciousness.

Dhyanyogi explained that young Anandi Ma was already highly evolved spiritually, and that if her parents would allow her to stay with him, he could help her control the divine energies pulsing through her and set her to work for the benefit of humanity. With her family's blessings, Anandi Ma left immediately for his ashram in Gujarat, where for three years she remained almost continuously in elevated meditative states. The meditation master who had worked for decades to help others raise their spiritual energy now struggled to help Anandi Ma lower hers so that she could function in the world. His respect for her spiritual power was so great that he instructed her to begin initiating disciples while she was still in her teens.

Dhyanyogi's own story is quite remarkable. He left home to adopt the life of a wandering monk at the hoary age of seven. After three decades of piecemeal practice, he met an adept who initiated him into the path of Kundalini Maha Yoga. This path traces its origins back thousands of years to Rama, the virtuous warrior king of Ayodhya. Rama initiated the next great master of this tradition, his wife Sita, who in turn transmitted the lineage to others. The most basic aspects of this yoga involve calming the breath and reciting the sacred mantras of the lineage. When the disciple's mind becomes completely tranquil, the guru transmits *shaktipat,* a transfer of consciousness/energy that in effect recreates the master's own state of spiritual realization in the receptive soul of the disciple. Through continual practice, students learn to stabilize themselves in this higher state of consciousness, eventually acquiring the ability to instill similar states in others.

Quickly maturing into an adept himself, Dhyanyogi devoted his life to teaching and to humanitarian projects. He is also widely respected in India for the famine and drought relief efforts he has organized, as well as for his spiritual eminence and longevity (he is presently well into his twelfth decade of life).

Then in 1976, at the invitation of American devotees, Dhyanyogi began teaching in the United States. With Anandi Ma (then called Asha Ma) at his side, he initiated thousands of Americans in the mysteries of *kundalini,* the current of subtle energy said to travel through the spine at the time of spiritual awakening. After establishing centers in Maine, Connecticut, and California, he returned to India permanently in 1980. Sensing, however, that Americans would continue to benefit from his teachings, he left Anandi Ma in the U.S. to carry on his work.

Anandi Ma's youth (mid-thirties), slight frame, and quiet demeanor belie her spiritual stature. Her silent presence in a room may easily be overlooked until she smiles and one sees the profound depth of spiritual experience reflected in her large brown eyes. She is accompanied by a relaxed looking Indian named Dileepji, who offers me fragrant *chai* (Indian spiced tea, steeped in milk) during my interviews with Anandi Ma. In 1980 Dhyanyogi recommend-ed that Anandi Ma marry Dileepji, who had been a devotee of his for 17 years, and that they continue the work together. Dileepji sits at Anandi Ma's side at all her public appearances; when her fledgling English fails her, she makes her point in Gujarati and Dileepji translates. Today as I put my questions to Anandi Ma, they adopt this team approach—Anandi Ma smilingly responds in her native language and Dileepji translates, occasionally adding insights of his own.

"I was wondering if you could tell us a little bit about what it was like for you as a child, growing up in higher states of awareness?" I asked. "Did your family realize what was going on? How did they relate to this when you were little?"

Anandi Ma nods, and speaks quietly in Gujarati. "One of the very strong feelings she had since early childhood was to become like a bird and fly away and not be attached to anything." Dileepji translates. "That was a very, very strong feeling she had almost constantly. That attitude kept her away from other routine things. She liked to be alone and quiet most of the time. As a result she didn't even do well in school; she didn't concentrate on her studies.

"Her father was very well versed in spiritual aspects, and in fact two months before all this started he had met Dhyanyogi and received *shaktipat*, so he had an understanding of what was going on with her when she started going into meditation and *samadhi*. He and the entire family were very supportive, but at the same time they didn't really know how to deal with it, and that's why Dhyanyogi was called in."

I couldn't help reflecting that if Anandi Ma had been born in the West and had those experiences, she would have been rushed to a psychiatrist. I asked how Dhyanyogi dealt with her.

"When Dhyanyogi first met her, already the flow of energy through her was profound. Her *kundalini* was very active and the force of the *prana* (vital energy) on the top of her body was very intense. In fact, he said if that continued it was likely that her body wouldn't remain. She wasn't functional at all on our level, so he had to work with her, bringing down the energy constantly so that gradually it would be more in her control. It took him almost three years; then he gave her mantras and certain techniques of yoga."

"Had Anandi Ma had any inkling when she was younger that she would become a spiritual teacher?"

"She had absolutely no inclination to be in that role, but Dhyanyogi said, 'The vessel is ready.' He was told by his masters from the lineage that she was the person to continue his work. It was not something of her own will; it was Dhyanyogi who asked her to continue to do the work."

I wondered what it was like to be personally trained by a renowned meditation master. I asked what Dhyanyogi was like. Anandi Ma's eyes shimmer with memories.

"When she left home for the first time and went to his ashram, the thing which touched her the most to start with was the way he greeted her. 'Where have you been all these years? I've been waiting for you!' And then his love, his caring, his simplicity, his softness—. The love that he gave was so unique and profound, she had never experienced that from anyone before. When she looked into his eyes it was like the infinite ocean. She felt that she should merge with that.

"During the three years that she was with him, she was touched by the care he took, putting everything else aside and working with her day and night. Sometimes she would be in meditation for hours, and it would take several hours to bring her out of it. This could happen any time, so there were many sleepless nights for him! His whole schedule was very much upset but he never got angry. Under the circumstances, anyone else would have lost their patience! From the simplest things to the major things, he was always concerned and took care about it. He was her mother, her father: her guru did everything for her."

"You were going off into higher states of consciousness. What are those states like? Everyone says don't even ask that question because there aren't any words to express such states of being. But when you were going into meditation, were you still conscious the same way you're conscious now? Was there joy, or was it beyond joy? What were you experiencing?"

Anandi Ma struggled for a few moments, searching for words, then spoke haltingly to Dileepji in Gujarati. He translated, "She says her first experience was in her home. They have a statue of the Divine Mother and she was chanting some *mantras*. All of a sudden, from the statue of the Mother there was a very brilliant, dazzling light, a thousand suns coming out, and then the Mother got absorbed in her. After that she lost consciousness. Since then she continued to have different experiences. She would see a form of the Lord and merge with that form completely and then she didn't have any consciousness after that. There are times when she's conscious of the experience afterwards, but basically it has to be experienced; it can't be described. It is beyond words because it's not of this world and not of this level of consciousness. That state is so unique that no one wants to come out of it. That's why Dhyanyogi used to take so long waking her out. The soul doesn't want to come out of that state."

"And yet, here you are. I'm very interested in this energy you and Dhyanyogi are working with." *Kundalini* is a subject that Western yoga students are fascinated by but I think hardly anyone really understands. I've read a number of books about it, and generally been more confused after I finished the book than before I started! There are lots of seminars on this topic, but I'm not always impressed by the credentials of the speakers. I am daring to hope that I will finally receive some clarification on this abstruse subject. A friend of mine, who spent his youth collecting initiations from various teachers, claims that the *shaktipat* transmission he received from Anandi Ma was by far the most potent and tangible initiation he ever received. If she truly is a master of these subtle energies, perhaps Anandi Ma can explain them in terms I can comprehend. "What is *kundalini* actually?" I plunge in. I add that sometimes people have odd or powerful experiences they believe signifies their *kundalini* has arisen, but I'm not convinced that's true.

Anandi Ma laughs, her dark eyes gleaming, but then she becomes very serious. "The *kundalini* is the part of the soul which comes before, and prepares the body before the soul can actually enter it. After the creation of the physical body is completed, it becomes dormant at the base of the spine. Yogis use that same energy to reach back to the soul, then to God.

"It is described as serpentine because of its motility, the way the energy moves. It lies in three and a half coils, which have several different interpretations. For example, it's said to represent the three aspects of creation: creation, preservation, and destruction; also the three qualities, *sattva, rajas* and *tamas:* purity, activity, inertia. It also refers to the three states of consciousness at different levels, what we know as the awake stage, the sleep state, and the dream state. And most of all it is *sat, chit, ananda,* what we call truth, consciousness, bliss. The half turn is the state we all should reach, known as *turiya,* completely beyond this level of ordinary consciousness.

"The *kundalini* is the mother energy, the *adi shakti* leading the person to the higher goal slowly and gradually. As a part of this awakening it brings about, so to say, some negativity as part of the cleaning process. That is what has caused some misunderstandings because people don't know how to deal with it. There is also a lot of misconception in that people may mistakenly think they have an awakened *kundalini*. We see many of those people as well. It is clear like day and night when the *kundalini* is awakened or if it is something else. Unfortunately in America because of the cultural background there is confusion, and the mind often is not willing to accept (the *kundalini* experience). It's not heard of in this culture and so people believe there's something wrong with them. That's the problem.

"You may know of the (involuntary) physical movements, called *kriyas,* that can be possible with *kundalini,* which are part of the cleansing. You will hear sometimes that there are injuries, and emotional things come out. Anger, fear, and such things often appear after the *kundalini* is awakened but those are very, very short-lived phenomena. It's just a temporary cleaning process; your *samskaras* (unconscious tendencies and desires) have to be released so that the mind is clear, in order for the person to evolve.

"Each individual will have different experiences because the past is different from individual to individual. In spite of all that, somewhere there is some sense of peace and joy at the very start. If a person can begin to relate to that and work on increasing that, the joy will become more and more until they reach the final stage, and then it's a permanent part of their being. That inner state of peace and joy is identical for all."

Anandi Ma sighs, and then continues, "Unfortunately here in the United States there are many people who are holding seminars and talking about *kundalini*. In India no one becomes a teacher until they are asked by their teacher to take over. There are very, very few people who really teach. They have years and years of practices and experiences. Then and then only they will venture about teaching. Teaching is the last thing that's in the mind. You have to be an expert in your field. Just reading a few things doesn't give you mastery on this subject. One needs not only years of practice and experience and the grace of the teacher, but also the grace of the lineage. That's the energy that's been generated for centuries, for millennia, an accumulation of hundreds of thousands of years of practice. When that is transmitted it makes a difference.

"It was written in the scriptures centuries ago that in this particular age [Kali Yuga, the Dark Age] the blind will be leading, and they're leading deaf people who don't want to listen anyway. So it's a bad combination. At least it's good that they're talking about *kundalini* and relating to it, but sometimes half knowledge is more harmful, leading people into strain, causing more problems.

"No matter what one is doing, if there is any spiritual evolution, it is the *kundalini* that is working within the person. It is the energy which helps you through the various experiences needed for individual evolution, and finally brings you to realization, face to face with the reality. In other words, the *kundalini* is like the rays of the sun. If you want to reach the sun, you follow its rays till you reach their source. That's the unity of Shiva and Shakti, rising and merging in the sublime *Sadashiva* (the ultimate, imperishable reality)."

A devotee of Anandi Ma's told me that one of the reasons he and his wife were attracted to her and Dileepji was because they're a couple. Many Indian teachers in the United States are, or claim to be, celibate. I'm impressed by the way Anandi Ma and her husband work as a unit. I ask if they would say something about their lives together.

"There's a belief that to evolve spiritually, one should be a *sannyasi* (renunciate) and a yogi, a celibate," Anandi Ma and Dileepji reply in a combination of languages. "But if you go into Indian spiritual history, you will see most of the great *rishis* (seers) were householders, they were couples. Their counterparts may not have been out in the forefront but many of the women were great yoginis themselves, and supported the yogis to come up to that level. Dhyanyogi always stresses that you should live in the world, do your normal duties, and yet you can evolve spiritually. For the cart to move forward, you need two wheels. There is more support in family life. That is the natural level of Shiva and Shakti—the union starts right there, in the Divine Being itself. Marriage is not only for physical life but also for spiritual support. It makes a big difference.

"Dhyanyogi always said that *sannyas* (renunciation) is not something external but an internal state of mind. When you are detached from everything, that is what *sannyas* is all about. Anandi Ma wanted sannyas but he told her, 'No, no, you live in the world and carry on. You are already a *sannyasi*.'

"The true sense of detachment has to come from the mind, not just from external behavior. You may give up everything and go to the forest to meditate, but if your mind is still in town, what is the use? If you live with moral restraint, you can still live in the world as well as evolve spiritually. Stay in the world. Maintain a balance.

"The other reason why he asked us to get married is that she still goes into deep states of meditation. Someone needs to wake her out with specific techniques, and I have been living with Dhyanyogi for 30 years so I am quite aware of all that. She occasionally goes back into those states, and it takes a lot of time and energy to wake her out. She cannot be left alone too much. In fact she would enter meditation in her sleep, so every morning she wasn't able to wake up on her own. She needed to be woken up with specific techniques. It's only in the last few years that she's beginning to wake up herself, but still there might be days when she might not wake up at all. So for that reason someone needs to be with her."

Watching Anandi Ma and Dileepji speak together is amazing: it's as if they're one symbiotic being. "I know in the Indian tradition it's considered that the husband and wife are one, almost literally, to the extent that the husband isn't allowed to perform certain rituals unless his wife is present. I don't want to overidealize things, but it almost seems like you two approach that oneness. You almost seem to know each other's thoughts."

The two exchange a bemused glance that seems to say the sort of harmony I'm picturing has not quite been fully actualized. Dileepji answers, "People get married for different reasons, to have children and what not, which is fine, but when the marriage has a goal of spiritual evolution, then the energy works at a much different level. We constantly have to think about others more than about ourselves."

I've been to numbers of Anandi Ma's public appearances and there's an issue I always hear being discussed as people leave the hall. Most Americans who're interested in yoga have already been initiated in some tradition. They may be very attracted to Anandi Ma but don't know if they can take the Kundalini Maha Yoga initiation without being unfaithful to their own guru. "Is it harmful to change gurus?" I ask. "Should we stick with the practices of one lineage only or can we incorporate some of the techniques you're teaching into our current practice?"

"That in fact is one of the disappointing things about our work in America," they answer. "People do tend to, what do you call, go guru hopping, going from teacher to teacher, take something from each. That is fine to a certain degree. It's perfectly valid as long as it doesn't add to the confusion of the individual. We always recommend that you should stick to one path and one teacher as your primary path, and then go to other teachers and learn whatever you can which will help your central practice, so that you can evolve. But what people tend to do is just say, 'Let's go to that ashram, let's go to see her,' and next weekend someone else is in town. They practice superficially so they don't benefit. If you are happy with the path and teacher and your practice, there is no need to do anything else, just stick to that. Just for purposes of *satsang* (spiritual fellowship) you go to listen to someone else. If something inspires you to do your practices in a much better and stronger way, that's fine.

"But the bottom line is that there are many people practicing different things, yet their *kundalini* may not be awakened. And at some point that has to happen, consciously or unconsciously. What Dhyanyogi always felt was let the person receive *shaktipat* so their *kundalini* is awakened. Whether he comes or practices doesn't matter. He's still going to benefit at some point because the principle of Kundalini Maha Yoga is that the *kundalini* itself moves you closer to the goal. No matter what he or she does, the energy will work. He kept it very open. You come or you go. If you want to receive the *shaktipat* he always gives the energy. Some people stick around for few months or years. Some we never see after *shaktipat* at all, they're gone forever. But at a subtle level the energy will still guide them and help them.

"The principle of Kundalini Maha Yoga is that once the energy is awakened through *shaktipat,* it remains active for three lifetimes. Within that period it will take the person to the goal for sure, by hook or crook as we say. That's why we see some people have major catastrophes in their lives, major accidents, or they lose someone they are very attached to. That's often the *kundalini* bringing about a rude shock that breaks the person out of their sleep, so to say. 'Hey it's time to wake up and start moving on.'"

"Kundalini Maha Yoga very much emphasizes the importance of the guru as the transmitter of spiritual energy. Yet in the past few years many Westerners have had bitter experiences with Indian guru figures, and the concept of uncritically laying oneself at the feet of the guru has been largely discredited." I ask Anandi Ma what a sincere disciple's commitment to a guru should be, and what is the guru's responsibility to the disciple.

"The chief role of the guru is to take the disciple to the final goal, no matter at what cost to himself or herself. They are responsible to help the person move along, remove the difficulties, and offer whatever help the person needs in the process of spiritually evolving. Even on a day to day routine level the guru will help the person evolve even if it is necessary, as the scriptures say, to give up his or her own life to help the person reach the goal. There are no other expectations or strings attached."

"Look at Anandi Ma's experiences with Dhyanyogi," Dileepji adds. "Oftentimes when she would be in pain and would be crying, Dhyanyogi would also shed tears. That was the interrelation of the pain between the guru and disciple. Despite all that he did for her and sacrificed for her, he never expected anything back from her except that she evolve and reach her goal. That is what is known as the *satguru,* the teacher that can take you to the final goal. There are different levels of gurus. Someone who teaches hatha yoga is also a guru, but cannot necessarily take you to the final goal. But he puts you on the road, so to say, gives you a start."

Anandi Ma says a few more words in Gujarati and Dileepji turns back to me. "Of course, for the disciple the requirement is to follow the teachings with great love and devotion. And again it is the role and duty of the disciple to take care of the external, physical needs of the teacher, their basic needs, whatever they need for a decent, comfortable life. It's like a father-son or a father-daughter relationship. In ancient times, of course, the disciple used to go and live with the guru in their home and the wife of the guru would take care of them as her own children. It was a completely different set up. Now things are different. Then the kings supported the gurus, because those were the only schools, so things have changed a lot.

"False teachers are not something new. This has gone on for years and years, not only in India but all over the world. Unfortunately in the name of something spiritual some people want to take advantage. People should be careful in what they get involved with, not just jump into things. There's the saying that before you accept a teacher, test them a thousand times. Only when you are satisfied that he or she is true and genuine, then you really accept a teacher. Once you have accepted, then no questions to be asked. Then you follow.

"Another thing to remember is that although the guru is false, the teachings they give, if they are from the scriptures, are never false. So if at some point people find out they were having a false teacher, they can leave the teacher but continue the teachings. On a subtle level often they are meant to get those teachings even through that false person. The teachings are meant for them, so they should continue with them, no matter what. If they continue with the teachings, they will reach the goal. There is no doubt about that.

"My understanding is that there are people who may come over from India who are evolved quite a bit but have still not reached the complete point. Western culture is such that it can pull people down if the person is not careful, and that has happened, from what we have heard. It's said in the scriptures, even after reaching a higher point, a person has to be very, very careful about falling downwards. There are a few who nothing is going to catch because they have gone through the process so deeply and elaborately, but in borderline cases they are likely to come down.

"It's written in the scriptures that there will be many false teachers in this day and age. They will prosper and there will be more people following them. True teachers will suffer more. It's a part of the energy of the age, so nothing can be done about it."

"As an Indian, you've been raised in an incredibly spiritually rich culture," I interject. "Dealing with Westerners, you're working with a very different type of student. I'd like to know what you see as the strengths of Westerners and also what you see that we need to work on."

"Dhyanyogi heard that another saint (Upasani Baba), who is no longer in the body, used to say that many souls from India were taking birth in the West. So there was some indication on the subtle level that for those souls to evolve, the teachers would need to come here as well. That's what prompted Dhyanyogi to come here. He planned to stay only for six months but after seeing the earnestness of the people and their strong desire to evolve, he decided to stay longer. Many people said, 'You're needed here in the West, so why don't you stay more?' In India people take these things for granted, although there's a much, much larger number of people who're really sincere and do tremendous things for their growth compared to the West. In the West, since information is lacking, people were so strongly desiring, and Dhyanyogi was moved to see that and decided to stay longer and help."

I asked if Anandi Ma found anything particularly frustrating about Western students.

"Nothing is frustrating, so to say, at the spiritual level, but due to cultural differences often times things are done on the part of the student which are not good for their own growth which we find frustrating. It's not their fault, but are the *samskaras* (psychological tendencies) which they have been given in their childhood. Even now in India, the entire culture is based on spirituality to start with so it makes a very, very big difference as the child is growing up. In the West we don't see as it as strongly as in India. So if someone wants to evolve, something comes in which holds them back, or that requires much, much more energy to break through. Often we feel we want to give but the person doesn't want to take. If he or she were an Indian, it would be much easier."

This raises an issue I and some of my fellow Western yoga students have wrestled with. Whether or not it's true that souls who spent many lives in India are now being born in the West, I personally find that I've been attracted to Indian philosophy and practice since my childhood. This draw does not always integrate neatly with my Western cultural views. "There's a part of many of us yoga students that wants very much just to go to the woods and do spiritual practice, but there's also a very strong desire to be successful in our jobs, to make money, to buy a nice house. It's hard to fit it all together."

"That's the *samskaras*. You have been trained as a child that to be successful in life you have to make all this money, buy the best car or the best house. This has been rooted in your mind since childhood and that has become such a strong *samskara* that to get that out is going to take a lot of effort. At the same time *samskaras* from past lives are saying you should evolve spiritually, and so you have to go off in the woods. That conflict remains, but again take the best of both worlds. Work hard and make money; there's nothing wrong with that. But you have all advantages here also. Whenever you can, take off to the woods and do practices. It's a little vacation whether it's two weeks or a month or whatever. In this country you have the facilities to do that, so besides your routine practices, set a time every six months or once a year or what works out for you, to just take off and do practices.

"The other thing is to pray to God to create the circumstances in your life where you can do the most spiritual practices. At some point those prayers will be answered. Things will just work out so easily that you will be able to have a nice, decent, comfortable life and at the same time do your practices to the maximum. We started small retreats in the United States Wednesday through Sunday. During those four or five days, we all sit together and do practices and chanting and meditation, and the outside world is forgotten. Even that short period of time will help."

"Sometimes it seems like there have been a lot fewer women teachers in the yoga tradition than male gurus," I bring up one of my pet peeves. "Lately however, it seems like there's a whole wave of great women saints emerging from India."

"Women teachers have been present all along, though maybe they haven't been out in public as much. Perhaps in current times it is through the female aspect that the spiritual energy is working more for the benefit of mankind. However, ultimately the gender of the teacher doesn't matter because, while the mind deals with male and female, consciousness itself is beyond that. For the soul there is no gender."

"As a woman teacher, do you have a special message for women yoga students?"

"We women should concentrate more on spiritual evolution and truly act as mothers for society. There is a tremendous energy within women that needs to be recognized and used for the welfare of the world. Women should begin by making the immediate family happy and peaceful, and gradually work outwards so that the entire nation can be happy and peaceful also. If they truly see themselves as mothers, then they can give pure, unconditional love to anyone. This is what the world definitely requires today.

"Pay close attention to raising your children in as spiritual and moral an atmosphere as possible. They are the roots of the future."

I ask Anandi Ma to summarize the basic tenets of her lineage.

"People should become conscious of their goal in life which is to understand and realize their true identity," Anandi Ma responds. "Through whatever means they like—it doesn't matter what path they choose—they should do something for their own evolution, whether it's Kundalini Maha Yoga or any other path. Whatever practices they adopt, do that with faith, regularly. They should remember that whatever they do spiritually is the root of life. If you water the roots, then the plant will flourish and there will be fruit. Otherwise, trying to do a million different things externally, making money, buying things, and all this, it's like putting water on the leaves but not the roots. The plant will not survive.

"Understand yourself. If you know who you are really, then you can truly give unconditional love. Once that begins to bloom within the person, and as more and more people begin to do that, we can change this entire earth. That energy will affect the family, from the family to the society to the nation to the world, but again the roots are spiritual practices.

"Lead a life, as Dhyanyogi said, that doesn't hurt others or yourself. Dhyanyogi said that India is the *dharma bhumi,* the home of religion, and America is *karma bhumi,* the land of action. When there is a unity of right action and *dharma,* then everything will be achieved. He said both these countries have a significant role for the world, and that's why there are teachers coming to the West. There's more openness to these teachings in America compared to any other country. At a subtle level, that energy is working, and as it increases things will be better."

"India is very different from what I expected," I admit. "It seems the image of India is very distorted in the Western press, so we have the impression it's all just poverty and misery. But it's wonderful! Even in Calcutta many of the people were healthier and happier than people in the West."

"That's true," Anandi Ma laughs. "That's the inner state of the mind in India, more content. Many sleep in the street but they sleep soundly. In America people have fancy beds but they have to take pills to go to sleep. In India they sleep in the street, but they'll be snoring away. There's a big difference between the two countries."

"Even the taxi drivers all have pictures of saints in their taxis!"

"That's what I mean about the culture. You come out of the airport, you get into the cab. Most likely there's a little altar right in the car, which you never see in the West. You have how many cars? In India as the child grows up, he or she is walking along the street and there are temples all over. Even if you don't want to think of the temple, but the *arati* (vesper) bells are ringing, automatically your mind goes there. The mind is constantly exposed to something spiritual, which doesn't happen with a Western child as much."

"Many of the devotees I met in Bengal do not do any particular *sadhana* like meditate," I comment, "but it's almost like they don't have to, because for them the Divine Mother is walking there in the street with them. They're so close to the Divine Mother. If we could achieve that level of devotion—"

Anandi Ma smiles and finishes for me, "—the battle is won."

§

"Anandi Ma is like Sita, wife of the avatar Rama in the Ramayana," comments a disciple as we sit chatting at Anandi's San Francisco Bay Area center. "Sita was very gentle, very quiet and loving—the shy face of the Divine Mother. I was there the first time Dhyanyogi made Anandi Ma appear in public in America. She was so shy she was crying. Tears fell on every bit of *prasad* (blessed food) she was distributing. I took the apple she handed me and tasted bliss. She has the *siddhi* (spiritual power) of Motherhood."

"I was determined to be a renunciate," laughs Mark Newman, who has practiced in this tradition since 1980. "Dhyanyogi introduced me to my wife Marsha." When Dhanyogi suggested they consider marriage, Marsha earnestly inquired, "But is that good for my spiritual growth?"

"When you are married," Dhyanyogi assured her, "your growth will go very fast."

Today Marsha and Mark have brought their 10 month old daughter to visit Anandi Ma. "I used to think education was academic," Marsha says. "Now I see it as exposure to great beings."

Ron Rattner, a lawyer initiated by Dhyanyogi 16 years ago, summed up his response to Anandi Ma: "It's nice that there seem to be more women teachers of promise—our society needs that. We need to come into touch with the Goddess within. Anandi Ma is teaching us how to do that in the best way possible: by example."

GURUMAYI CHIDVILASANANDA: BEAUTY AND GRACE

A tantric scripture states that initiation by a woman teacher is eight times more effective than by a male. Although this may or may not be literally true, there is undeniably tremendous power in the archetypal figure of the mother/virgin/guru. This is especially evident at the worldwide Siddha Yoga centers, where Gurumayi Chidvilasananda has presided since the passing of the enormously popular meditation master, Swami Muktananda, in 1982.

"When Baba Muktananda died, I was shattered," recalls one Siddha devotee. "Who would be my teacher? It's all over, I thought. How could Malti (Gurumayi) possibly replace Baba?" Siddha Yoga is based on the transmission of spiritual power through the guru, and now the guru was gone.

"I knew Malti when she travelled with Muktananda as his English translator," the devotee continues. "She was one of us—she went to movies, she ate pizza. She was skinny and shy. How could she be the guru? I left for several months, and when I came back and went up to see her and she bopped me with her peacock feathers, I looked up into her eyes and couldn't believe it! It wasn't her anymore. It wasn't Malti—it was the guru. The guru was coming through her. She had become Gurumayi, our Guru Mother."

Muktananda was an ardent devotee of *chit shakti*, the feminine principle of the universe, which he described as "the soul vibrating in the heart. (Her) manifestations—as the world and as the Self—are both filled with bliss and beauty." He was one of the few Indian teachers to offer *sannyas* (monastic vows) to women, whom he honored as embodiments of the Goddess. Shakti, he wrote, "appears as woman. . . . (She) takes the roles of daughter, housewife, mother, yogini, genetrix." His explicitly-stated desire was that all the world's women would "see the *shakti* glowing within" and perceive her great glory as their essence.

Muktananda backed his benedictions with action, passing his lineage, and thus control, over more than six hundred Siddha Yoga centers scattered throughout fifty-two countries to Yogini Sri Malti Devi, a young Indian devotee whose development he had guided since infancy. Malti shaved her head, donned the ochre robe of a renunciate, and received the monastic name Gurumayi Chidvilasananda ("filled with the guru, the blissful play of consciousness"). Though she originally shared leadership with her brother, the twenty-seven year-old Gurumayi was formally installed as sole head of the Siddha Yoga Dham on November 10, 1986.

Many of the students at today's Siddha centers never met Muktananda. They were attracted not by the aging yoga master—whose classic autobiography, *Play of Consciousness*, galvanized thousands into taking up the practice of yoga during the 1970's—but by his young protegée, whose stunning beauty and disarming humor have melted the hearts of many a skeptic. Gurumayi's teaching emphasizes not so much the philosophical abstrusities of Kashmir Shaivism (Muktananda's spiritual heritage) as the practical disciplines of spiritual life and the joy of loving and serving humanity.

"We are not trying to conquer the world or convert people," Gurumayi explains. "There is only one thing we want to do—to keep spreading that love as much as possible. Let us spread that one thing which is so sweet, so tender, and so tangible, a love that is pure and that can take us where we really want to go—to the heart, where God dwells."

In her efforts to spread this message of love, Gurumayi often undertakes a grueling itinerary: her world tours include free programs throughout Asia, Europe, Australia, and the Americas, along with extended retreats at her two main centers in South Fallsburg, New York, and Ganeshpuri, India. She appears almost nightly, a schedule that would exhaust the most hardened road musician, yet she appears fresh and buoyant at each stop, chanting,

Photo courtesy of SYDA Foundation, Oakland, CA.

teaching, and then sitting for hours to greet devotees who file up to meet her.

Public lectures form only part of her outreach; Gurumayi also makes a point of visiting devotees in their homes and businesses. During a visit to Northern California, devotees in a Bay Area neighborhood known for its high concentration of Siddha Yoga students were asked to hang white flags in front of their houses if they wanted their guru to stop in. Gurumayi strode down the streets, stepping into each devotee's home to offer a blessing. One mail carrier, puzzled by the large, well dressed crowd scurrying along the sidewalk, followed into an apartment. I had to laugh at the photograph of the astonished looking postman sitting among dozens of devotees before one of India's greatest Shaivite masters!

Wherever Gurumayi appears, advance teams of devotees transform rented auditoriums into magnificent meditation temples, full of flowers and portraits of great saints of the Shaivite lineage. The air crackles with expectation as "old timers" and "newcomers" gather to meet the woman whose "one look, one word, one thought, one touch" can transform their lives, according to the Siddha literature. Is this all hype, or can Gurumayi actually transmit *shakti*—spiritual energy—as the tantras declare a handful of advanced adepts can do? I am at Siddha Yoga's Oakland, California ashram tonight to find out.

Although I have arrived an hour and a half early, admission is by no means assured: twelve hundred bodies are crammed into the hall, where people are asked to sit on the floor very nearly in each other's laps so that space is not wasted on chairs. Even with these draconian measures, outside the main entrance hundreds of would-be participants are regretfully turned away; there literally isn't room for one more body.

Stepping through the ashram entrance is like plunging into a ocean of sound: a thousand voices are simultaneously chanting the Siddha mantra, *"Om namah Shivaya"* ("I honor the inner Self"), and the atmosphere is celebratory. Gurumayi, clad in the ochre robes of a swami, enters the room, and a devotee hands her a stringed instrument. As she strums the ektar and sways rhythmically, Gurumayi's deep, resonant contralto guides the chanting to a crescendo. Some devotees coyly wave their arms through the air as if they were antennae directly absorbing the energy they believe is emanating from their guru. The music stops, and Gurumayi joins her palms before her heart as she salutes the audience: "With great respect and love, I welcome you all with all my heart."

Gurumayi begins to teach in her typically lucid style: "We've come here not because we already know the Truth, not because we already know God, but to go to a place within ourselves. To strengthen this state within, we gather here summer after summer. Talks will be given only for you to go inside. No matter what happens, there's one goal: the experience of devotion, the experience of love. . .

"As you do your practices, there is an opening. This entire universe is the pulsation of God. In this pulsation, there is opening and closing, opening and closing. As you do your practices, you experience the opening, and not the closing. The whole universe opens itself for you."

Gurumayi encourages us to open our hearts through the traditional Indian practice of chanting the names of God. This advice makes me flinch. As a child I was asked to lip synch as my enthusiastic but atonal rendition of the music at hand was spoiling the experience for others present. I have not sung out loud in public in fifteen years. As if she had read my mind, Gurumayi relates that once while a small group was chanting before her guru, Baba Muktananda, a particular devotee was way off key. Gurumayi, who is a superb singer, began chanting louder to try to cover the cacophony. Noticing that Muktananda was frowning, she wished the tone deaf woman would have enough respect to keep quiet.

After the program Muktananda demanded, "Why did you sing so badly today?" Gurumayi was taken aback because her own singing had been technically perfect. Pointing at the woman who could not carry the tune, he continued, "Why can't you sing like her?" With a shock Gurumayi realized that the guru was much more impressed with the other woman's whole-hearted abandonment to the chant than with her own musical proficiency. Laughing at the memory, Gurumayi assures us that the One to Whom we are singing is listening not to the notes from our mouths, but from our hearts.

The hall darkens and a harmonium begins to play. Gurumayi initiates the chant: *"Kali Durge namo namah!"* ("To the Supreme Goddess I bow again and again!") I join in tentatively. Gradually I note, with some satisfaction, that a few of the women sitting near me are just as approximate in following the melody as I.

And then the chant swallows me. It is coming not from my mouth but from the root of my being. *"Kali Durge! Kali Durge!"* Like a thousand other voices in that dark hall I am suddenly singing perfectly—and at the top of my lungs. I am a wave in an ocean of mantra as we cry out the Divine Mother's name over and over again. It is ecstactic: I am singing here, filled with bliss, and then I am gone. All that remains is the Inner Observer relishing the *nada,* the vibration, of the Goddess' name.

Abruptly Gurumayi ends the chant and we are plunged into a silence so deep that not even thought disturbs it. The experience is awesome. Perhaps when the Siddha devotees claim their master can give one a glimpse of one's deepest self, this crystalline state of lucid serenity is what they mean.

There are many charismatic leaders who can drive their audiences to a state of fervor. It is a rare one who leads her listeners to this state of perfect silence.

Gurumayi's devotees say she is a *siddha,* a perfected master. I would concede she appears to have the *siddhi* (yogic power) to create *Svarga*—heaven on earth—wherever she goes. In 1987 Gurumayi received the key to the city of Oakland, local officials' token of appreciation for the Siddha guru's impact on the high crime rate, crumbling neighborhood in which the California Siddha ashram was established. Devotees renovated the area, rebuilding and opening businesses like Amrit, Siddha's gourmet vegetarian restaurant.

Gurmayi's ashram in Ganeshpuri is so extraordinary an oasis that as you enter the grounds from the suffocating Indian plain, you literally feel the temperature drop several degrees; it is as if someone had turned on an air conditioner. In fact, under Gurumayi's direction devotees have planted a veritable tropical forest of beautiful plants in the parched Maharashthan soil that actually alter the microclimate. The temples, auditoriums and statuary are opulent even by American standards and immaculately maintained. The setting is so lavish it is almost unearthly.

The South Fallsburg ashram in New York state is similarly eye popping. The reincarnation of an old Catskill Mountain luxury resort, it includes an auditorium with plush blue upholstered seats and sparkling chandeleirs. Walking across the estate with devotees in expensive suits and elegant, calf length dresses, I begin to feel uncomfortable. Are my clothes stylish enough? Is everyone noticing that it's been too long since I cut my hair? Noting the life-size photographs of Siddha masters on the wall of the auditorium, none of whom appear to have owned more than the loin cloths they were wearing, I wonder aloud if Gurumayi is taking Siddha Yoga in a direction the *siddhas* themselves would not have recognized.

"Yuppie yoga?" my guide laughs. Then she becomes quite serious. "There are many people here who never were attracted to spiritual life till they met Gurumayi. She's created an atmosphere where they can feel comfortable—clean and beautiful and very

Western in some ways. They feel at home here; they feel respectful. When they see this ashram they want to clean and beautify their own lives."

It occurs to me that many of us yoga students are children of Sarasvati, the Goddess of wisdom. We forget to acknowledge others who may be children of Lakshmi, the Goddess of prosperity. Almost every other ashram I have visited in the United States is struggling month to month for its financial survival. At the Siddha centers, however, it is not unprecedented for wealthy celebrities to make million dollar donations. Gurumayi honors beauty and wealth, and they pursue her wherever she goes.

Most Western yoga students are oriented to the ascetic traditions of yoga, and may be unaware that other types exist. Once, while researching the Dasha Mahavidyas (ten great schools of Goddess worship in India), I thoughtlessly let slip a derogatory comment about the amount of money it must have taken to furbish a particularly ornate temple. The brahmin priest yanked me off my high horse immediately. "The Goddess is beauty and wealth. Prosperity is a gift of the Mother. We should be grateful. When we make the temple beautiful, we honor her. When we make ourselves beautiful, we are showing our respect for her.

"Everything the Mother has created is beautiful. We should follow her example and make everything around us beautiful. Beauty raises our minds to the highest. It gives us a glimpse of the truth. In India we have a saying, 'Satyam shivam sundaram.' It means that God is truth and truth is God, and that God is beauty and beauty is God. God, truth and beauty: they are the same. The most honored name of the Goddess is Maha Tripura Sundari. It means 'the Supreme Beauty in all the Worlds.' When you have beauty you don't even need yoga and meditation. Beauty itself takes you to the highest. Beauty creates in you the state of meditation spontaneously. Therefore we worship the Mother by making the temple beautiful. When the temple is beautiful, the Supreme Beauty comes here to reside. When we make our hearts beautiful, she goes there to reside." Duly chastened, I decided to leave my self-righteousness outside with the rest of the dust and the dirt.

Wealth does not ensure special perquisites here, however. All residents are more or less randomly assigned *seva*, work duties that range from cooking the sumptuous vegetarian meals to cleaning the bathrooms to cutting the grass. *Seva* is the great leveller of devotees, regardless of age, ethnicity, or financial bracket, and can make or break a would-be devotee's stay at the ashram. "*Seva* means selfless service," a devotee explains. "It's a powerful spiritual practice—just as powerful as chanting or meditating. During *seva* you have to apply the inner peace and love you've experienced in Gurumayi's presence. You have to stay calm when you're assigned a job you totally hate, like having to wash dishes while Gurumayi is giving a program. You have to see that scouring the toilets is just as much a service to the guru as taping a video program. Baba Muktananda always told us to see the divine in ourselves and each other. During *seva* we practice seeing the divine in each other while we work together.

"Sometimes people leave because they can't stand the *seva*. They want to be with Gurumayi but they don't want to work. But if you can't work with an attitude of love and servicefulness, what kind of a spiritual person are you? What have you really learned?" Gurumayi sets the pace: the number of hours she spends per week serving her students is staggering. Yet watching her stroll around the grounds, advising visitors and supervisorsing construction projects, I'm amazed at how relaxed she seems, as if being the spiritual guide and ultimate role model for tens of thousands of Siddha devotees around the planet is the easiest and most natural thing in the world.

A small crowd surrounds Gurumayi, eagerness and anxiety alternately playing across their faces. Gurumayi seats herself on a bench, as beautiful, elegant and unstrained as a spring flower, and casually begins to tease a teenager sitting near her. Residents assure me that although Gurumayi's interactions are always loving, they are not always easy to take: her expectations for Siddha students are high, and those who are not measuring up quickly hear about it. "Gurumayi believes in self-discipline. Even with the best guru in the world, if you don't have self-discipline you won't achieve anything spiritually. When she sees us failing in our discipline, she lets us know. That can be really painful, but it also shows how much she cares. It's scary and it's amazing the way she always seems to know where I'm at spiritually and emotionally, even if I haven't talked with her in weeks."

Gurumayi's own service activities include massive acts of charity. The poorest of the villagers in the Ganeshpuri region are fed and clothed through the largess of the ashram. Medical volunteers from the West tour Maharashtra offering free exams, medicine, and eye surgery for cataract sufferers. Siddha Yoga is not about amassing wealth but about spreading it around.

Gurumayi, who in some ways is perhaps the most savvy of the Indian women saints I have met in her comprehension of Western values, is also a stalwart supporter of the higher aspects of her own culture. Traditional Indian music and dance are fostered at her ashrams, and brahmins are regularly imported to South Fallsburg to conduct *pujas,* ancient Vedic rites. Tonight they will be conducting a ceremony in celebration of Nava Ratri, a ten-day-long festival honoring the Goddess. Having had the opportunity to visit many Indian temples, I unfortunately must report that at many of even the most holy sites in India, *pujas* are conducted in a lifeless and perfunctory manner. The priests are clearly more interested in collecting a fee than in creating a sacred atmosphere. In Gurumayi's presence, however, the *puja* becomes pure magic: one is transported back thousands of years to an era when the *devas*—the "bright beings" who inhabit the heavens —responded to their supplicants' invocations and descended to receive the offerings of coconut and rice which the priests toss into the sacred fire.

But perhaps that era never actually ended. Gurumayi steps up to the fire pit, lifts a large brass pitcher, and pours *ghee* (clarified butter) onto the flames. They leap toward her fingers as if asking for more. The brahmins, bald but for one thick lock of hair falling backward from their fontenelles and clad only in a cotton cloth draped around their waists, chant mantras handed down from prehistoric times. Suddenly the clouds in the sky, the wind in the trees, the fire roaring before us, all seem to take on life, and I wonder if the *devas* are among us still. I am not just being poetic: the sense that we are surrounded by numinous beings is positively uncanny and heightens as the ritual progresses. Perhaps it is the all-pervading nature of our own numinous being that we sense.

Gurumayi's striking beauty rivets attention wherever she goes. She has the face and figure of a fashion model; on her the simple orange robe of a renunciate looks like it was designed in Paris. She is so thin that I worry about her health, yet her energy seems inexhaustable. Her grace, delightful wit, and respectful regard for the needs of each devotee have expanded Siddha Yoga's appeal beyond what even Muktananda achieved. Her male devotees worship her—indeed, I speak with a half dozen who are obviously smitten: she is the spiritual ideal and the unobtainable, inviolable love. But women also respond to her overwhelmingly positively. Her wisdom and strength are qualities to which many of them aspire.

Does Gurumayi have a special message for women? "It's just her example," explains Janet Dobrovolny, a California attorney. "I was brought up to understand that I could do anything I wanted to do. A lot of women weren't. It's a very great thing to see a woman with that level of attainment. This experience helped give me the inner strength to set up my own law office. She's very supportive—she's visited my office. She has the women more involved in management throughout the ashram. Seeing her gives us women that extra bit of confidence, that extra bit of grace that some of us particularly need since women still tend not to shoot as high as men.

"It's time to bring more a balance to our spiritual lives," adds Dobrovolny, "to bring more of the feminine in." Gurumayi is facilitating this process at many levels. "More women are coming out as spiritual teachers now that Gurumayi has been around for a few years."

Does Gurumayi have a special appeal for women because she's female? At almost any Siddha Yoga gathering in America, women outnumber men three to one. "In India, though, the men outnumber the women," answers Swami Radhananda, another woman ordained by Swami Muktananda. "The greatest appeal is not that she's a woman, it's simply because of who she is—an increasingly great spiritual teacher."

Gurumayi is one of the few popular Indian teachers who has taken a stand against the sexual abuse of women disciples. A high-ranking swami whose sexual adventures were compromising his role as a teacher was asked to step down. This painful and embarrassing episode may ultimately have served a higher purpose: besides reflecting Gurumayi's personal courage and integrity, it signals a clearer sense of responsibility for a spiritual teacher's actions and is perhaps a harbinger of the sorts of reforms that will be instituted as more and more women assume leadership roles.

When next I see Gurumayi in Oakland, thankfully, the venue has been changed from the beautiful but cramped ashram to the Paramount Theater in the heart of the city. Even in this huge arena with its multiple tiers of balconies I am lucky to find one of the last empty seats. The program begins like a sales pitch: devotees file onto the stage to offer testimonials to the life-transforming effects of Siddha Yoga and center leaders encourage the audience to sign up for weekend intensives during which the actual transmission of *shaktipat* is said to take place.

But if it's not *shaktipat* that's occuring right now, as Gurumayi walks onto the stage, I don't know what else to call it. Love, perhaps. The intense feeling of the huge crowd for their teacher surges forward and Gurumayi lifts her arms, almost as if she is physically buoyed by it, and reflects it back.

Gurumayi does not give interviews; indeed her personal life, to the extent that she has one, is carefully shielded in order to preserve the mystery of the guru-disciple relationship. Because of this I am a little suspicious, and scan her face for any betrayal of arrogance or boredom. Though I risk being accused of hagiography, I have to report that I honestly cannot see any. Gurumayi genuinely loves these people. She takes her role as their spiritual mentor extraordinarily seriously. It is not for self aggrandizement—and certainly not for fun—that she's going to be sitting on that stage for the next eight hours, trying to inspire her devotees to maintain the rudimentary spiritual practices that so many of us pay lip service to and so few of us actually do, and then listening for hours to devotees' hopes and fears as they step up to her for *darshan,* their moment to speak with her or simply accept the blessing she bestows with the touch of the peacock feather wand she gracefully plies. She is here to serve them.

Gurumayi has a relaxed method of lecturing which creates the powerful illusion that she is speaking to me personally. She seems psychologically incapable of giving a dry talk; her speeches are laced with easy humor that completely disarms the listener till she drives her often deeply profound point home. "There is a dog trainer in South Fallsburg," she begins, and describes the trainer who worked with the ashram's massive, puppy-like guard dogs. He didn't like to see the dogs running freely, getting excited. It made them difficult to discipline. "Don't let your dog get all worked up—then it's too late," Gurumayi quotes, flashing another of her brilliant smiles. "I always felt this was a great teaching."

What do we do when we get "all worked up," caught up in our emotional agendas, slipping off the path once again? "Don't worry about making amends. Just begin where you left off. Don't worry about the goal, just keep going." The previous night California switched to Pacific Daylight Time. "Don't worry about getting ahead; you're already an hour ahead." Everyone laughs. "There's always a traffic jam in the mind. But there is something unruffled by all your thoughts. Think about it.

"Very few people remember how precious life is. Seize hold of the moment before you to begin your journey to the universe within you. However many times you falter, seize the moment again and again."

Whether they know it or not, Gurumayi is leading her audience to the truths of Kashmir Shaivism. This tantric school, popularized by the sage Vasugupta in the 8th century A.D., is described in abstruse texts like the *Shiva Sutras* and *Spanda Karikas.* For centuries scholars have wrestled with these scriptures, yet Gurumayi explains their tenets so clearly a kindergartner can understand. She tells the story of the dog who stumbles into a hall of mirrors. Seeing itself surrounded by other dogs it becomes frightened and bares it teeth. A thousand other dogs simultaneously bare their teeth. Terrified now it starts to bark. A thousand dogs start howling. Attacking the mirror, the dog is attacked by a thousand enemies and dies of fear.

Later a sage walks into the same hall of mirrors. Everywhere he looks he sees himself. The sage smiles at this spectacle of his all-pervading nature and calmly walks away. "All these creatures we see are not different from pure consciousness, they're just contractions of pure consciousness," Gurumayi explains. They are reflections of the reality that lies within ourselves. "A pure mind is a mirror of God. A good mind creates a great universe!"

I continually feel as if Gurumayi is specifically addressing my own psychological issues, like my maddening judgmentalism. "Great beings are not blind to the faults of others, but they are not burdened by them either. They see the greatness in them also. Treat people as if they are what they ought to be—without expecting a commission! You give them the power to be what they have the ability to be.

"Then be the person you want others to be."

I don't feel that Gurumayi is feeding us time-worn truisms. These words, when she speaks them, carry incredible power. It is as if she is sharing her own innermost spiritual secrets, the very methods that transformed her from Malti the pizza aficionado into a *jagad guru*—a world teacher.

From Gurumayi's point of view however, the transforming power was her guru Muktananda. "O my sweet Muktananda! Seated within, it is you who make me say all this," she confesses in *Ashes At My Guru's Feet,* her spiritual autobiography. To her he was no mere eccentric *sadhu* in an orange woolen cap. "Was he ever born? Or did he always exist?" She sees him the same way he beheld his own mentor, the legendary Nityananda of Maharastha, as the *guru tattva,* the grace-bestowing power of God. Like a ripple being carried across the sea on a swelling wave, the Siddha devotee merges his or her mind in the vast ocean of the guru's consciousness, which carries it to God.

The kind of spiritual and psychological surrender this process entails is no less than a form of personal immolation. Obviously this is a path many Westerners would refuse to take. In the West this image of total surrender immediately conjures pictures of Jim Jones and David Koresh. Lacking living examples like Anandamayi Ma or Sarada Devi, we find it hard to believe that individuals pure enough to accept the gift of our faith without twisting it to their self-interest could possibly exist. Even in India would-be disciples are advised to examine a prospective guru closely, for years if need be, before making this kind of life commitment.

Across the globe, hundreds of thousands of devotees have examined Gurumayi, and found her a teacher of exceptional spiritual and ethical standards. They have taken up the Siddha Yoga practices like chanting the lengthy *Guru Gita* each morning and constantly remembering the Siddha mantra *Om Namah Shivaya*. They are not asked to renounce the world, but rather to live as if the world and all its denizens are redolent with God. And again and again Gurumayi takes pains to explain that the guru's blessings these practices evoke are in reality the grace of their own higher nature. She and the other masters of the Siddha lineage are human symbols for an enlightened understanding which ultimately they will have to find in themselves. The external guru can point the way, guiding and inspiring, and even administering doses of *shaktipat*, but success can only be assured when the devotee applies that unavoidable flip side of grace: sincere effort.

According to the tantric scriptures, loving and serving an authentic guru gradually creates a sort of telepathic connection between student and teacher. Then when the disciple reaches a point where no further efforts avail (a point clearly described in the yogic literature), he or she "surrenders" and the *shakti*, the consciousness-power of the guru's awareness, carries the devotee "to the other shore." What one experiences there, the texts say, words are powerless to describe. However, it is critically important to select an authentic guru, because only one who is "there" can take you there.

I myself cannot certify that any of this is true. I can only say, observing Gurumayi's complete immersion in *muktananda*, "the bliss of perfect freedom," and the extraordinary majesty and serenity this appears to have given her, that it looks as if it may be possible.

Ma Yoga Shakti:
No Nonsense Yogini

I first glimpse Ma Yoga Shakti playing the harmonium in a Hindu temple and singing earnestly of Shiva, the God of universal transformation, who sits in meditation at the summit of Mount Kailash in the Himalayas. "When I was very young I was taught to do prayers to Shiva. Since childhood he's been my God," she explains, pushing the hand organ away. I am a little intimidated by Ma: although a tiny woman of 65, she exudes an aura of command not unlike a spiritual drill sergeant. Her face radiates intelligence and clarity but also a deep purposefulness that doesn't brook frivolity.

Though she is an orange-robed *sadhu* (wandering swami) now, Ma Yoga Shakti led a full life before taking formal vows of renunciation. She raised a family, completed a master's degree in Political Science, fought for women's rights in India, and established a women's college in Bihar. Today she is the spiritual director of ashrams in Bombay, New Delhi, Calcutta, and Madras, as well as in New York and Florida.

"A sadhu needs only two things: two pieces of bread and *satsang*," Ma Yoga Shakti announces as she begins the *satsang* (gathering for spiritual fellowship). For a brief moment, the entire temple brightens as she smiles. Referring to the fact that some Indian *sadhus* feel they also need *bhang* (hashish)—in fact there are legends that Lord Shiva himself indulged—she continues brusquely, "Shiva is not allowed to have *bhang* in my ashram. Sometimes people makes excuses for weaknesses in the name of God." I have no doubt that in Ma's presence even Shiva would hesitate to light up.

"Everyone wants to rise high. This is a desire God places in your mind, a demand for enlightenment. The souls wants to grow." Ma launches into the story of how Vindhyachal (the Vindhya mountain range separating north and south India) envied the Himalayas because they were so tall. So Vindhyachal performed severe penance in order to achieve the power to grow extremely rapidly, and as a consequence rose higher and higher every day. Finally the Gods became worried that Vindhya might ultimately block out the sunlight, endangering all life on earth. They went to Brahma, Vishnu and Shiva—the greatest of the Hindu Gods who admitted they were helpless against such tremendous penance, and explained that only a human being could forestall a crisis. "God fills your mind with inspiration but doesn't run after you with a stick. Humans are supposed to handle their own affairs," Ma pauses to explain.

So the Gods appealed for help to the elderly sage Agastya. "Agastya was a *rishi*, a realized soul. *Hri* means heart, and a *rishi* is one whose heart is filled with light. The *rishis* live always in the *satya yuga*," the golden age in which truth always prevails. Agastya agreed to help. He crossed the Transhimalayas in one year, the Himalayas in two years, and came at last to the Vindhya mountains.

Now Vindhyachal started worrying, "If I don't show respect to this great seer, he may curse me," so the huge mountain range bowed low, allowing Agastya to clamber over. Having reached the other side, the sage blessed the mountain range for its thoughtfulness. "When you humble yourself you receive blessings," Ma interrupts herself to comment. "Respect knowledge and you will be happy."

"Vindhyachal, can you do me one more little favor?" Agastya asked innocently. "Anything!" the mountain range eagerly responded.

"Please remain low until I return. I'm very old and it will be difficult for me to climb back over you if you become too high."

Vindyachal happily agreed but, as everyone knows, Agastya never returned to North India. After all these thousands of years, he lives in the south still. That, of course, is the reason why, to this day, the Vindhya mountains are not very high.

"America has grown like Vindhyachal," Ma Yoga Shakti continues for the benefit of the Americans present. "The gods are

overburdened with happiness, like children in America. Who has time to enjoy all the channels, all the food, all the Coca Cola? America also needs a lesson in humility to make it sweet. It needs, like the Vindhyas, to learn to bow low in service."

Ma pointed out that the Goddess was so pleased with Vindhyachal's behavior that she came to the Vindhyas to live. I had to smile, imagining her perhaps one day setting up shop in the Rockies!

"East and West are like two arms. Both together can uplift the world. West paid more attention to material prosperity. East paid more attention to inside. But now modern science has brought all people together. That is also God's work.

"There are good and bad everywhere. You've been given the right to choose either. King Parakshit wanted to destroy evil all together but evil said, 'I'm also a child of God.' Those things which appear wrong are not evil but are meant to promote our progress. All problems are our tutors; they accelerate our efforts to find God. If you believe in God, nothing is a problem."

Ma is enjoying herself. "These are divine stories—we could talk all night. You don't need wine when you tell these stories, you feel intoxicated. In India nobody cares for TV, they're happy with chanting and meditating, singing and chanting. You can't purchase this joy in shops. By singing the glories of God you make your heart free."

Ma Yoga Shakti meets with me at the home of a devotee. As a *sannyasini*, a Hindu nun, she has no home of her own but moves continually between her ashrams, temples where she is invited to speak, and devotee's houses. She is difficult to interview. Any Indian would know that it is inappropriate to ask a *sannyasini* questions about her personal life. When a Hindu takes formal vows of renunciation she literally performs her own funeral service and assumes a new name; two strong symbolic statements that the old personality is dead, and a new life wholly dedicated to spiritual realization and service has begun. Ma flatly refuses to talk about herself but I persist, finally convincing her that the story of her own evolution might benefit others.

Ma's interest in spiritual life began early, she reveals. She learned yoga the way most women in India do: through the oral tradition, passed down by one generation of spiritually motivated women to the next. "I learned everything from my grandmother. She was illiterate but I have not seen anybody as wise as she was. She used to get up at three o'clock and chant. She was reciting the

Bhagavad Gita, she was discussing Ayurveda, she was always making medicines. She was the director of the whole household."

Ma imitated the *pujas* (religious rituals) her grandmother faithfully performed before the family altar. "As a little girl I thought, What is this? Why do I have to clean these utensils (for *puja*) every morning? But later on I understood it is your mind that has to be cleaned."

That was as much as Ma Yoga Shakti would say about herself; the conversation turned to more general topics. I admitted that I had not realized that formal vows of renunciation were available to Hindu women. "In India we have a long tradition of independent women *sannyasinis.* They have always been." Throughout history a small percentage of women have refused to accept the role assigned to traditional Hindu females, and have left their homes to go on pilgrimages or settle into forest shacks or mountain recesses to practice yoga.

At the 1974 Kumbha Mela in Hardwar (a major Hindu religious festival attended by as many as 30,000,000 pilgrims) Ma Yoga Shakti was given the title Maha Mandaleshvar; she is the only woman of whom I am aware who has been granted this honorific in recent times. It literally means "Lord of the Great Mandala" but its connotations are very complex. A common practice of Indian yogis and yoginis is to worship a *mandala* or *yantra,* a geometric design whose every line, angle, circle, and petal represents a particular Goddess. Each Goddess in turn is the symbol of a specific divine power or quality such as creation or destruction, heat or cold, love or wisdom, hatred or jealousy. (Yes, negative qualities and emotions are also seen as part of the divine play in the Indian tradition.) Through intense concentration on the Goddesses of the *mandala,* and repetition of the mantras associated with them, the worshiper unites with and finally masters the powers they represent. Therefore to call a woman a *mandaleshvar* is a poetic way to acknowledge that she has mastered the *mandala* of her own mind and body, that she has mastered herself.

Ma Yoga Shakti is an advanced yogini. In the West we tend to think a yogini is a woman who has become particularly adept at *hatha* postures. This is not at all the meaning of the term in India. *"Hatha* yoga is only a preliminary practice to keep the body healthy. There are four steps of yoga. First is *karma* yoga, second is *bhakti* yoga, third is *raja* yoga, fourth is *jnana* yoga. They are not different paths; they are one and the same. First you solve your daily problems, *karma* yoga. Be efficient, expert in your daily work. *Bhakti* means you purify your emotions, your heart, your mind. Then you are a good person in the family and in the nation also. When you love God, you love his creation also. Creation is a manifestation of God's glory."

In *raja* yoga, one sits for meditation. Ma typically sits for five hours. Ultimately the meditative state should persist whether one is sitting erect with eyes closed or working busily in the world. "If mind is always in control, every second, that is called *sahaja samadhi.*"

Jnana yoga is often translated as the yoga of knowledge. Ma quickly clarifies: "Liberation is not intellectual. Intellectually you can't understand it. The intellect is helper and intellect is barrier also. One is bound by nothing else but his own mind. It is the quality of your mind that makes you feel bound or liberated. Body, mind, and spirit should be in harmony with each other. The spirit should speak through your intelligence and intelligence should direct your actions. It is all one."

Ma's comments remind me of the story of one of the most famous yoginis in India's vast body of mystical literature. Ma Yoga Shakti herself recounts the tale of Queen Lila in one of the books on yoga she has authored. Lila had been very happily married, and the sudden death of her husband plunged her into spiritual crisis. "What is death? Does my husband still exist? Is there any way to contact him?" She began to meditate and, strongly motivated by grief, quickly achieved the state of one-pointed concentration that is the goal of yoga.

Sarasvati, the Goddess of Wisdom, was impressed by Lila's sincerity and rapid progress in meditation. She revealed to the queen the consciousness of her late husband, which in its after-death state was enjoying a heaven of its own creation, a wealthy new kingdom the monarch believed he was ruling, complete with his own imaginary version of Lila! Then, to impress on Lila how the worlds of life and death are both filled with *maya*, Sarasvati also showed her her past and future lives which, from the Goddess' perspective, were all occurring simultaneously! Finally Sarasvati guided Lila across an unimaginably vast, freezing void to worlds circling other stars. There Lila saw other humanoid creatures, as well as civilizations of entities more like what we would call plants on our own world, and beings so strange that, the text says, "even the yogis don't understand what they are!"

I can't resist asking Ma if the story of Lila is wholly metaphorical, or if advanced yoginis might actually be able to move through the universal mind as Lila does.

"There is time within time, space within space, mind within mind. There are different dimensions of living. The human body is not equipped to perceive everything. There could be other places also, just like cats can see in the dark but our eyes cannot see. The universe is very complex. We are all children of infinity. Where are babies coming from? Where are people going to (at death)? There could be many dimensions of creation, and there are."

The Goddess teaches Lila that the material world is ultimately no more real than the worlds of our dreams; both are the products of consciousness. Though Ma Yoga Shakti relishes this story, what she teaches her students is much more practical. "You have to plan your life yourself, be responsible. It is your life. You can make it or mar it. To make yourself happy, first solve your own personal problems. Then go out and help others. Good people are always in demand.

"Yoga is the best tool to help people. Practice *karma* yoga, *bhakti* yoga, *raja* yoga and *jnana* yoga. We have all enjoyed the facilities of society. Then in return it is our duty to give something back, to leave a better world behind. I ate the mangoes grown by others. Now I must grow fruit trees so that others can enjoy.

"The world is one family. We have to feel that we are all one. We have to share the sorrows and the joys, both. We are all responsible for the sorrows and joys of the world. Yes, I am also responsible for the sorrows. Therefore I do more chanting, more penance. May all be happy! I believe that the world is our family, yoga is our way, knowledge is our breath, and service is our worship.

"Even one little practice makes us so high. I don't think I have done much, but only a little practice has given me so much that I can't handle it. Yoga is a secret science. It enlightens your mind and you can't believe the power. But misuse can be there. So practice *satya*, be truthful always. *Ahimsa*, never think of hurting anybody, even your enemies.

"The first mantra and message and wisdom teaching of the Vedas is 'Everything here is permeated by divine energy. God is everywhere in all forms. Nothing is bereft of divine energy. Do not renounce that energy but enjoy it without greed.' One condition is laid there, don't be greedy."

Does it get lonely, I wonder, a lone woman wandering the world, telling divine stories and singing the praise of Shiva?

Ma Yoga Shakti laughs. "I don't feel isolated ever, anywhere. The world is my community." It strikes me now that when a *sannyasini* symbolically immolates herself during her renunciation ceremony, she is not really losing anything. Instead she gains everything. When Ma leaves forward to tell me, "We should be loving and caring for each and every one. God bless you," I feel the potency in her words, a power that comes from words lived, not merely spoken. Perhaps that is why the Indians call her Ma Yoga Shakti, "mother of the divine energy of yoga."

As I leave Ma's presence, I recall a favorite yogini story of mine. It is actually an ancient myth of the Goddess Parvati, "the daughter of the mountain," which explains why the Goddess resettled in the Vindhya mountains. A demon had acquired the power to defeat every enemy except the son of Shiva, which made him invincible, since Shiva, the supreme yogi, was an ascetic and had no intention of ever fathering children! The fate of the universe was in jeopardy as the avaricious demon overran the worlds, so the Gods decided to send Parvati, the most voluptuous young Goddess imaginable, to seduce Shiva and hopefully produce a divine son.

Parvati tried every feminine wile in her repertoire, but absolutely nothing would arouse Shiva from his meditation. Finally Kama, the God of Lust, attacked Shiva with a powerful flower arrow. One of Shiva's three eyes fluttered open. Parvati hoped she could finally catch the great ascetic's attention—till she saw Shiva blast Kama to ashes with an angry glance from that third eye! The great ascetic immediately resumed his meditation.

At this point Parvati faced an inner crisis that changed her forever. She saw that she could never seduce Shiva, yet she could not return home after having failed the Gods. A tremendous sense of disgust with the affairs of life surged in her heart. Then and there Parvati decided to renounce the world. She traveled to the Vindhya mountain range, covered herself with the ashes emblematic of a renunciate, and sat down to meditate. Years passed, but Parvati did not stir. She was absolutely determined to achieve final liberation.

Deep in his meditation, Shiva began to sense an extraordinary shakti, a divine energy more powerful and sublime than anything he had ever experienced before. To his shock he realized that it was a growing field of consciousness as perfect and extensive as his own. What could possibly be the source? He opened his three eyes and there on a distant peak he saw a yogini sitting immovable as the mountains themselves, covered with dust, her mind merged in the absolute. In that instant the great renunciate and lord of all yogis fell madly in love.

From their homes in the heavens the Gods smiled, foreseeing the imminent divine union that would give birth to a savior. In saving herself, Parvati had saved the world. In mastering herself, Parvati had mastered *shiva,* a Sanskrit word that means "the supreme auspiciousness." Ma Yoga Shakti's own example reveals that today women are still walking away from their old definitions of themselves and from the roles society requests them to play, even when they can play those roles successfully. They are heading for a higher ground, a summit of new understanding, and the arms of divine love. When they achieve their goal they bring a new force into the world, that of the truly enlightened life. I think of Ma spending the last years of her journey absorbed in Shiva, and I hope I can close my life as auspiciously!

Ammachi:
In the Lap of the Mother

"Worldly love is not constant. Its rhythm fluctuates; it comes and goes. The beginning is always beautiful and enthusiastic, but slowly it gets less beautiful and less exciting. In most cases it ends up finally in upset, hatred and deep sorrow.

"Spiritual love is different. The beginning is beautiful and peaceful. Then comes the agony of longing. This pain of love will prevail until it leads to unity with the beloved. This unity in love remains forever and ever, always alive, both within and without, and each moment you live in love. It will swallow you completely until there is no 'you.' There is only love."

She knows what she's talking about. The speaker is Amritanandamayi Ma, a diminutive, semi-literate South Indian from a small fishing village by the Arabian Sea. She grew up in abject poverty (even the sari she wore had been loaned to her), the victim of years of physical and psychological abuse. Sudhamani ("Pure Jewel," her birth name) attended school through the fourth grade, when her mother's illness forced her to remain home to attend to the household. The work load was enormous for a nine year old, but Sudhamani's mind was absorbed in Lord Krishna. If she suddenly realized she had taken several steps without remembering Krishna, she would run back and walk those steps again, repeating the Lord's name.

Sudhamani's unconventional ways were particularly irritating to her brother, who was so enraged by her refusal to marry and her adamant insistence that she would take up the spiritual life, that at one point he actually attacked her with a knife. Throughout this harrowing childhood she practiced *karma* yoga, deliberately surrendering every thought and action to God.

Later in her girlhood, Sudamani felt the call of the Goddess. She would walk to the seashore at night and, like a drop merging with the ocean, merge her heart in the fullness of the Divine Mother. Villagers would find her apparently unconscious on the beach, totally absorbed in the Goddess. While this makes for an inspiring story in retrospect, it had a less salutary effect on her family at the time, who had little patience for these "fits," and less for the coterie of devotees who began to gather around her. Sudamani reached adulthood before her family finally grasped that they had a bona fide saint on their hands, and that the crowds gathering at their doorstep were not going to get any smaller.

In the past decade, millions have come for a glimpse of the holy woman from Kerala. When Ammachi ("Darling Mother," as the Indians affectionately call her) appears in public, thousands stream out of their villages to receive her blessing. She is what the Indians call a *mahatma,* a great soul. The embodiment, they say, of absolute, unconditional love.

When I saw Amritanandamayi Ma in India she was surrounded by over 20,000 devotees. Having just completed a program of devotional singing, she was taking time to greet her devotees personally. All of them. The evening passed, then the night, then the morning. There was not a trace of strain or fatigue on her face, and only 5,000 devotees left to go. Beaming her blessings at the enormous crowd, she touched every person who came to her, was completely present with each one, and pressed *vibhuti* (sacred ash) into their palms.

Is this for real? I wondered as I limped away from the tumult, my legs aching from sitting so long on the hard ground. The experience left me with a much deeper appreciation for the quality control standards Indians apply in gauging their mahatmas.

In the past seven years hundreds of thousands of Americans and Europeans (and lately, Russians) have joined me in marveling at this 40-year-old woman, since Ammachi has been travelling from Zurich to Tokyo to Chicago, offering her gift of inspiration to all who attend her free programs of song and prayer.

To those of us yoga aficionados who have heard it all, Ammachi has nothing to say: speaking no English, she doesn't talk at all. Instead, she just is what she is. She speaks through her eyes,

reaching out to embrace each astonished American or Australian or Swede who shuffles forward, rubbing our backs and slipping us chocolate Kisses. For many Westerners, this unlikely meeting is galvanizing.

The balding gentleman sitting across from me in the large San Francisco church where Ammachi is greeting visitors, has been weeping for hours. Later he confesses, "My God, I haven't cried like that since I was five years old. When Ammachi lifted my face and looked in my eyes, and I saw that perfect, pure love, I just lost it. I didn't know such love existed."

Since Swami Vivekananda's arrival in the United States 100 years ago, most spiritual teachers from India have been lecturers, and have stressed the practice of yogic techniques. The God-intoxicated mystics, like Vivekananda's guru Ramakrishna, tended to stay at home. Ammachi's mission does not seem to be to reiterate that through concerted practice we can reach *sahaja samadhi*, the state of continual absorption in divine consciousness, but rather to show us what that state actually is.

Ammachi's tactic of refusing to deal with Westerners on a verbal level is brilliant: it forces us to come to her as she comes to us, from the heart. It strips us bare of our manipulative strategies; we are inarticulate children again, at the feet of our mother. Maternal and solicitous, radiant in her simple white sari, Ammachi wipes away the tears that flow spontaneously from many of those who have come here to meet her. Accepting an infant offered by a young father, Ammachi bounces the baby on her lap, laughing and teasing it affectionately. Everyone here is her child. She has the widest lap in the world.

Although Ammachi never got as far as the fifth grade, today scholars sit at her feet. Like India's recent sages Ramakrishna and Anandamayi Ma, who were also barely literate, Ammachi speaks from the depths of her own spiritual experience. For a woman with no guru and no formal religious training, her understanding of Vedanta, Tantra, and the intricacies of yoga is prodigous.

Fortunately, many of her conversations with devotees have been recorded, and translations of her teachings are now available in English. One pilgrim who crossed the backwaters of southern India's verdant tropical forests to reach Ammachi's ashram, hidden by coconut and palm trees from the sea some yards away, asked her what path of yoga is most appropriate for Westerners. After demurring that each individual is different and should be guided directly by his or her own teacher, Ammachi offered a general answer.

"The path of devotion is the best for Western children. In the West, society is such that people, even from early childhood, take an intellectual approach to everything. Their analytical minds are well-developed, but their hearts are dry."

"What can we do about this dryness?" wailed the pilgrim who, like me, understood all too well what Ammachi was getting at.

"First, develop one-pointed love towards God. When that love becomes the center of your life and as the devotional practices become more and more intense, your vision changes. You come to understand that God dwells as pure consciousness in all beings, including you. As this experience becomes stronger and stronger, the love in you also grows until at last you become that. The love within you expands and embraces the entire universe with all its beings. You become the personification of love. This love removes all dryness from you. It is the best cure for all emotional blocks and negative feelings.

"Reasoning is necessary, but we should not let it swallow the faith in us. We should not allow the intellect to eat up our heart. Too much knowledge means nothing but a big ego. The ego is a burden, and a big ego is a big burden.

"Haven't you seen people who stand as guards for somebody else's property like a paddy field or a wealthy man's estate? When these guards talk to someone, they will pose as if the whole thing belongs to them. Scholars are like that. The real owners are the ones who have realized the inner wealth through meditation."

While the Sanskrit language and traditional Hindu scriptures are taught at Ammachi's main ashram near Trivandrum, the value of book learning is kept in perspective. "Children! Can one live in a drawing of a house? Can you enjoy sweetness by licking a paper on which 'molasses' has been written? If you see a billboard advertising a jewelry shop in Kanya Kumari, can you purchase gems from the billboard? Of course not! Dear ones, just so you cannot experience bliss merely by reading the scriptures.

"Devotion without knowledge cannot free us, but knowledge without devotion is like eating stones. On the path of devotion we can enjoy the fruit from the very beginning, experiencing bliss in every action. In other paths, this occurs only at the end. We can get fruit from the jackfruit tree by picking it at the base, but in the case of other trees we must climb to the top to reach the fruit." The bliss that comes from higher states of awareness cultivated through years of rigorous penance is freely available at any moment to those who love God. We have only to open our hearts.

But how can we ordinary mortals pry our self-centered hearts wide open enough to let God in? "Real love arises only when all attachments to individuals, objects and personal interests drop away. Then the battle of life becomes a beautiful play. It becomes selfless service extended toward the entire human race out of compassion. In that battle it is not your ego that is fighting, but love that is consuming your ego and transforming you into love itself."

Many teachers emphasize the importance of love, but Ammachi's words have a particularly potent impact on so many who have met her because they see that she walks her talk. "Ammachi gives all the time, twenty-four hours a day," reports a devotee who has known Ma for six years. "She lavishes her love freely on everyone who comes to her. She may be firm with them, but she always radiates unconditional love. That's why people are so shaken after they meet her. She's a living example of what she teaches, of what all the scriptures teach. She sets an example for the rest of us. It's incredibly inspiring. No one believes that what she does is possible till they see her doing it."

"Ammachi doesn't just lecture on yoga; what she does is model for us the state of continual divine intoxication and overflowing compassion," a secretary from Marin agrees. Unlike many saints who recoil from contact with ordinary people, Ammachi embraces the masses. "Many thousands of people come to cry on her shoulder," a disciple explains, "and she hugs and consoles them. She says that of the thousands who have come to her, very few have had anything happy to say. She says the sorrow of the world is immense."

"There are many ashrams where they will teach you how to become enlightened," Ammachi says, but she herself prefers students who not only seek union with God but are also deeply committed to serving humanity. At the same time Ammachi is a yogini after the old school: she demands strict discipline on the part of her close disciples. I myself find the program of *tapas* (spiritual austerity) that she prescribes for the *brahmacharins* (celibate disciples who live with her) quite intimidating. It stipulates eight hours of meditation daily in addition to constant social service activities. Ammachi herself does not sleep more than two hours per night, and her disciples hardly have time to rest either. Asked if this routine was also expected of her lay followers, Ammachi responded:

"Mother does not like to use the word *tapas* because it scares many Western children. They think *tapas* involves physical and mental torture. They are afraid that through *tapas* they will lose all their desires, and they do not want that to happen. They want to enjoy life. The only problem is they have a wrong idea of 'enjoying life.' Real enjoyment depends on relaxation, not on tension. Yet most people are very tense all the time. Men are not able to spend any peaceful moments with their wives and children. They are more worried about their work, their business, their status in society and about what others will think or say about them. They want a new house, a new car, a TV, or a new relationship. The modern man is fed up and bored with old things. His mind is always set on what he does not have. He is always living either in the past or in the future, never in the present, and he runs after everything he craves. He has no time to enjoy, to relax, and be in the present. Finally, he collapses.

"But you can turn your home into a haven, an abode of happiness and bliss. There definitely is effort involved; it can be a kind of *sadhana*. It is all right if you want to call it *tapas* if that helps you think of it as a serious matter.

"The present way of living will only end up in greater distress and sorrow. The problem is you. It's within you, not outside. If you really want to enjoy life, try this path of mental disciplining and see what happens.

"A *griham* (house) is an ashram or hermitage. That is how the word *grihasthashrami* (householder) came into being. A *griham* can be converted into an ashram. An ashram is a place where people devote all their time and energy to the remembrance of God, doing selfless service and developing qualities like love, patience and respect for others. They do spiritual practices to help them see unity in diversity. First, they fill their own hearts with love, and then wherever they go, this love is expressed in all that they do. They see beauty and harmony everywhere. Family life can also be like this. That is why a householder devotee is known as a *grihasthashrami*, a person who leads an ashram life while remaining in his house. He or she is a person who tries hard to attain the supreme goal, bliss, even while living with their spouse and children. This is possible if you sincerely try."

Impressed by the quality of renunciation they see at Ammachi's ashrams, women sometimes come to Ammachi believing they must leave their husbands to take up spiritual life. "Mother tells them, 'Why are you throwing him away? Serve each other. In this age it is not appropriate for everyone to renounce the world,'"a devotee reports. Ammachi teaches men to see their wives as the Divine Mother and women to see their husbands as the Lord of the World, and also to serve their families, the community, and the world. Humility and service are her constant themes.

If she is to succeed in spiritual life, Ammachi specifies, "some of the qualities of a man, like detachment and courage, should be assimilated by a woman. Ladies are not generally interested in renouncing worldly life to attain God. Who would keep creation going? But if their interest is kindled, then they can make even faster progress than men."

Basking in Ammachi's love is a wonderful experience, but for students who want to continue the work of self-transformation, Ammachi highly recommends the practice of raja yoga. "The ancient masters thoroughly studied the human mind. They penetrated into it and understood its subtleties. It was only after such exhaustive study that they have written down all the disciplines that a spiritual aspirant should observe. Today everyone writes a book. But Mother wonders what study they have done about life and their mind.

"The *rishis* (seers) were not superficial. They spent days and nights foregoing food and sleep to study their mind. The result was the attainment of ultimate knowledge. They knew well the obstacles that a *sadhaka* will have to confront during his spiritual journey because they themselves had faced them."

Nevertheless, "however much we meditate and do *japa,* it is of no use if there is no love for God. A boat travelling against the current will inch its way along no matter how hard one rows, but if a sail is tied, the boat will pick up speed. Love for God is the sail which moves the boat forward."

Yoga students who complain that they do not have time for the spiritual practices Ammachi prescribes: *dhyana* (meditation), *japa* (rememberance of God), *kirtan* (devotional singing), and *seva* (selfless service), receive a blunt response: "If we want to be more honest and sincere with ourselves, it would be better if we were bold enough to admit, 'I'm not interested in spiritual matters,' rather than twisting the truth by saying, 'I have no time.' When we really have the desire to do something, time and the proper conditions will be at our disposal. Time and circumstance follow desire."

I spend some time talking with Neal Rosner, Ammachi's first Western disciple. He had spent twelve years as a monk at the late Ramana Maharshi's ashram in Tiruvannamalai, when a friend persuaded him to visit the then little known woman saint from Kerala. Ammachi advised him, "You have been treading the path of knowledge for a long time and still have not achieved what you set out to accomplish. Why do you not try crying to God? You may be able to succeed in that way."

"How is it possible to cry without reason?" Neal equivocated.

"Take a photo of your guru and, keeping it next to you, weep to him to reveal himself to you and rid you of all your sorrow. Just try it. It is not as impossible as you think."

After Ammachi left to visit a devotee on the other side of the island, Neal tried to eat, but each time he raised the spoon to his mouth, he would burst into tears. Ammachi's image was indelibly imprinted in his mind's eye. His friend Chandru was deeply alarmed; these emotional outbursts were entirely uncharacteristic of Neal. "It's taking her a long time to return. I'll sit outside and chant my mantra," Chandru said. "Wherever she is, she may hear me and return immediately."

Sometime later Ammachi's mother came rushing in. "Ammachi is coming," she announced breathlessly. "We were on the other side of the backwaters and could not get a boat to take us across. Ammachi started to shout, 'Chandru is sitting there in the hot sun and Neal is weeping to see me. If you do not find a boat soon, I am going to swim across!'"

At that moment Ammachi walked into the room. "Crying?" she asked innocently.

I mention ruefully that in this country many seekers have had far less benign encounters with spiritual teachers, and feel leary of uncritically embracing any new teacher who arrives from India, no matter how loving they may initially appear.

"One should observe the guru's conduct, their life, their history, their teachings to see whether their life is reflected in their teachings, and the other way around also," Neal thoughtfully responded. "In the West people are very credulous and feel that if they're having so many experiences when they go to spiritual teachers, it means the teacher is great.

"With Mother, I find that the way she was when I met her twelve years ago when nobody at all knew her except the villagers, and the way she is today, is the same. Her total lack of worldliness is the same. If you had seen Mother fifteen years ago, before she had any contact with society, you would call her an *avadhuta*. An *avadhuta* means someone totally beyond this world, beyond the physical plane. You would say they're crazy. They have no standard of anything. You used to find Mother lying in the backwaters in Kerala, in the water and mud, or dancing under the trees at night. She would eat off the ground, whatever anyone would give her. She was dead to her physical existence. I've seen this with my own eyes. Many times she'd be sitting out in the sun in *samadhi* and it would start raining—you know the tremendous monsoon rain—and she wouldn't move. If you're in an airplane you don't feel like walking on the ground. That's Mother's condition.

"There was an *avadhuta* in another part of South India that we once visited and he was most offensive. He was spitting on Mother and no one could understand what he said. He was really dirty. He used to sit in one corner and that was his whole life. When we came out of the room we were so angry, we never wanted to see the fellow again. But Mother just kept sitting in there. Finally we got in the bus and she just smiled and said, 'He's really in the supreme state.'

"Everybody in unison said, 'Oh! If that's the supreme state I don't want anything to do with it!' And then she said, 'None of you can understand it. And I can't explain it, but when you're in his state you'll understand why he's like that.' That kind of sums up Mother's inner life. We can infer so many things but unless we get in her state ourselves we can't understand what it is really."

"Mother did not use to wash or brush her teeth or bow in the temples," brahmacharin Ramakrishna adds. "She was beyond those things. But then some of the devotees, who were not beyond them, began to imitate her. Only then, for the sake of setting an example, she changed her ways, and began following the social norms."

"You can see the rest of Mother's life right in front of you." Neal continues. "Whether it's a woman or a man or a child or a rich person or a poor person—they're all the same to her: she's the mother. Everybody's a three year old child before her. That's how she sees everybody. And that's not just words. She makes us feel what we really are. We really are children of the Divine Mother, but as we grow up our mind gets hard and we get angry and proud and jealous—we become an adult. We lose our innocence. But Mother says that you have to become a child again if you want to realize God, if you really want to be happy. Christ said the same thing."

Ammachi is from Kerala which is a Communist state. I ask Neal how the authorities have dealt having one of India's greatest living saints in their midst.

"They're changing a lot. All of Kerala is changing because of Mother. People had lost faith in God; they gave up their religious traditions, mostly because of Communism. And now thousands and thousands of people are changing because they see Mother, and they're convinced that she's the Divine Mother. If she goes somewhere outside the village, you can be sure there will be 15,000,

20,000, 25,000 people who see her in each place. People have been craving for a real saint, and they see that's what Mother is."

Ammachi makes no claims to being a divine incarnation; she insists instead that she is "the servant of your servants." "I want people to worship God, not me," she has repeatedly stated, yet throughout South India I met people absolutely convinced she is an avatar.

"They feel that she's more than a saint because she's been like this since she was a child." Neal explains. "They feel that she's an incarnation of the Divine Mother. Traditionally it's told that you can tell a person is an *avatar* if in their childhood they realized God, they use their realization for the good of the world, that they're born masters, and they had no teacher. This is very rare."

The day Ammachi first set foot in Moscow (August 17, 1991), Soviet Communism collapsed. The symbolism of this coincidence struck me very powerfully. There has long been a strong Catholic tradition that Russia would be liberated by the Divine Mother.

Interestingly, when brahmacharin Chaitanya frankly asked Ammachi, "Are you God?" the ashram reverberated with the peals of her laughter. Referring to herself, as usual, in the third person, she replied, "Amma is a crazy girl. The only reason Amma is sitting here now is because no one has put her behind bars. Amma does not ask anyone to believe in her. It is enough for you to believe in yourself."

"There have been other inspirational teachers in the West who have offered unconditional love to their audiences." I mention to Neal. "The last time I saw one of these he looked terrible, as if he were on the verge of collapse. I assume it was because giving and giving just burned out his nervous system. Yet Ammachi keeps giving, one on one, not just to hundreds of people but to tens of thousands at a time, and she always looks fresh and joyful. How does she do it?"

"She says she's equipped for that job. That's why she was born. She compares herself to a sweeper, a person who cleans up all the rubbish and then afterwards goes for a bath. She knows how to take a bath, not physically but in her own way. Not everybody knows how to do that; they know how to give but they may not know how to get rid of what they're taking.

"It's unbelievable, I mean her batteries are not like our batteries. She goes and goes and goes and we collapse. If you live with her you're exhausted all the time. Mother comes home at four in the morning and then she reads letters till five. Finally she sort of dozes off and then may wake up an hour later and off she goes again.

"We lived in one hut together for the first two years of the ashram. There was Mother and me and Swamiji (Amritswaru-pananda). I could never do that again! That was the most difficult thing I've ever done, living in the same room with Mother for two years. The light was on all the time because she'd never sleep. And always people in there, always she's very boisterous and lively—she's so full of energy and life. That room was like a circus all the time—always *satsang* (spiritual fellowship). Fortunately we got a second hut."

"Years ago I was sitting in the hut in Vallickavu with the other devotees, enjoying Mother's presence, when suddenly I noticed a terrible stench," relates another of the brahmacharins. "I turned around and saw a leper walk in, completely covered with oozing sores. You cannot imagine the smell. I almost vomitted. Mother jumped up and ran to him, her face shining with joy as if a long lost child had just returned home. She embraced him and fussed over him and washed his wounds with her own hands." At this point the story takes a more shocking turn—confirmed by several witnesses I spoke to who were with Ammachi during this period. "She asked him to come again regularly, and every time he came in, she would lick the pus out of his sores. Over the months the leprosy disappeared. Only one small sore remained. When we asked Mother why she didn't heal the leprosy completely, she said, 'As long as the disease remains, he cries to God. If the disease is completely removed, he may become complacent.'"

Miraculous stories are told of all India's myriad saints. I personally find these tales charming and inspirational although—I'll be candid—I don't take them literally. However, while it's easy to shrug off purported miracles by historical figures long dead, it's discomfitting to hear life-transforming personal experiences related by credible witnesses sitting across the table from me.

One young man relates that Ammachi was talking with a group of devotees in Vallickavu when she abruptly turned and commanded him to return home immediately, even arranging for a car to speed his journey. He rushed home to find his mother weeping before Ammachi's picture on the family altar. "I was leaning over the oven when I felt an excruciating pain in my heart," his mother explained. "I knew that I was going to die. Suddenly I thought of you, and knowing that you were at the ashram, I prayed to the Holy Mother, 'Please send my son back to me so that I can see his face one last time.' I fell unconscious to the floor, but woke up some time later, astonished to be alive. I smelled Holy Mother's fragrance, and as I slowly opened my eyes I saw her sitting next to me. She was holding my heart medication in her left hand. 'Yes daughter, you took the medicine. Be at peace, you are all right,' she said. Then she vanished. I jumped up and searched for her everywhere but she had disappeared. Still her fragrance permeated every room in the house. I returned to the kitchen and the pill bottle—which I keep locked in my medicine cabinet—was lying on the floor."

Listening to the Indians earnestly relate many such impossible experiences with Ammachi, I am struck by how differently they view the universe. In our culture the Goddess is a feminist symbol of self-empowerment, a political icon with dramatic political and philosophical resonances. In India, however, the Goddess is *real*. From earliest childhood these people have listened to scriptures like the *Chandi* in which the Goddess promises that whenever her children are threatened or go astray, she will incarnate to save them. The Divine Mother is not a concept to them; she walks their streets, she abides on the altars they build for her in their homes. When they look at a *mahatma* like Amritanandamayi, they actually see the Mother of the Universe moving among them. I leave it to the psychologists to explain the psychosomatic mechanism that allows this kind of faith to create apparent miracles.

I had the opportunity to observe the ancient tantric *kanya kumari* ceremony in a Hindu temple, in which a three-year-old girl was dressed and worshipped as the Goddess. My interest was originally anthropologic, but as the ritual progressed I found myself falling powerfully under its archetypal spell. The rite is also often conducted with adolescent girls, as well as with very elderly women. The great nineteenth century saint Ramakrishna worshipped his wife Sarada in this manner.

I arrive at the Mata Amritanandamayi center near San Ramon, California, having heard that Ammachi will be conducting a similar rite, called the Devi Bhava. I find many people I know here today, devotees from the Sai Baba ashram, from Ananda, and Self Realization Fellowship, from the Siddha Yoga center. There are Christians and Buddhists and Jews, all sectarian loyalties laid aside to greet a saint whose embrace is universal. The huge auditorium is so full that last minute arrivals cannot squeeze in the door.

When Ammachi enters the hall many devotees bow before her, and instantly my "cult alert" sensors start to blink. Except, if this is a cult, why is no one pressing me to join the organization (it turns out there is no organization to join), why is no one trying to convert me to their theology (before the worship begins I am told to visualize whatever aspect of God I am most comfortable with, and if I don't believe in a personal God, to imagine the formless reality), or, most surprisingly, why is no one pressuring me for a donation? A brahmacharin explains that Ammachi abhors the modern tendency to turn spirituality into business, and has forbidden her disciples to ask for money. There is, however, a booth at the back of the hall where cassettes of devotional music and exquisite Indian jewelry are being sold for the lowest prices I have seen in this country. One hundred percent of the proceeds are used to support the orphanage, schools, medical clinics, vocational training institutes, hospices, and homes for widows and battered women, which Ammachi maintains in India.

In the next moment Ammachi is on all fours, pressing her forehead to the floor. For a full minute she bows to the divinity in us. I am caught completely off guard: I personally find it distasteful to bow to anyone else, and here this world-renowned saint is bowing to me! This reminds me that in India the significance of prostrating is to show respect to one another's divine nature, not subservience.

The program begins with *Devi Puja,* an ancient South Asian rite in which the Goddess is propitiated for the benefit of all beings. Waving spoons of flaming camphor and chanting *Om Parashaktyai Namaha* ("Homage to the Supreme Primordial Consciousness/Energy"), we follow Ammachi's instructions as she speaks through Swami Amritswarupananda. "Mother says the masculine principle has overtaken the world and that is what is causing many of the problems today," he translates. "We must bring the nurturing energy of the feminine back into the world. That is why we are worshiping the Goddess today." We offer flower petals symbolizing all our hopes and fears, one by one, to Parashakti, the Great Mother.

After a vegetarian dinner, the *Devi Bhava* itself begins. The curtain is drawn back across the stage, revealing Ammachi as we have not seen her before. She is draped in a stunning sari, decked with jewels, and wearing a silver crown. To Westerners, unfamiliar with this type of rite, she has explained, "Children, when we see the dress of a postman, we are reminded of letters. Likewise, Mother's dress is to remind you of the Supreme. The world respects only the dress. The visual appearance of Mother in *Devi Bhava* is to release us from our limited perception of our Self and remind us of the Supreme which is our true nature."

She is in *samadhi,* a state of intense meditative concentration. Like the *kanya kumari* rite, this ceremony allows us to symbolically enact the experience of being in the presence of the

Mother of the Universe. This ceremony is so radically different from anything most of us have experienced in our own culture, that I am frankly astonished no one walks out. Instead, people line up to approach "the Goddess," to make physical contact with the divine. For many of the individuals here, that moment leaning across the Goddess' lap to receive her blessing is one they will cherish their entire lives.

"It's something instinctively felt by the people, in spite of the cultural difference that they see there," Neal Rosner comments. "It's not on a mental level that they feel it at all. It's entirely intuitive. It's something that they can't put their finger on but it's so true and it's so deep in them. People love it so much because it's coming from the core of reality."

I cling to my cynicism. It is both my sword and my shield. From my teen years investigating paranormal phenomena, to my adulthood exploring various spiritual paths, again and again I have been impressed by our immense capacity to delude ourselves. We are credulous creatures; we want to believe, we want life to be magical, to be spiritually meaningful. Too often we confuse our interpretation of events with the events themselves. Then when something untoward occurs, like a sudden death, we are stunned. For an instant we hover at the brink of that terrifying abyss of stark reality the Hindus call *Kali*. Then immediately we scramble to find meaning in the event, to make excuses for God's apparently capricious will.

I have always been attracted to saints and their inspiring teachings, but in "real life" I work at a major research university, and am daily exposed to fresh neurophysiological data revealing that much of what we believe is psychic and sacred in ourselves is in fact biologically mediated. Yet standing in the presence of a phenomenon like Ammachi, I feel my well-ordered, thoroughly documented version of reality begin to crack. I find myself asking new, incredible questions. Is it possible yoga isn't just about stretching into a pose, or enhancing one's clarity and creativity, that it actually can be a door to another dimension of being that expands out infinitely not only beyond the intellect, but beyond human imagination? That love can be more than a comfort zone or a social palliative; that it might be a vehicle into the very heart of God? Burned out on the hype about gurus, I resist "surrendering" to spiritual authority figures, yet some part of me wonders if it might be true, as Ammachi suggests, that "The guru is the embodiment of pure consciousness. There is no person there. He simply is, and you benefit from his presence. If you really want to use the guru, then surrender to your own Self. It is the same as the guru's Self."

I inch my way toward Ammachi's chair, where she sits blazing with love. One after another, two thousand people are coming forward to lean into her lap and be embraced and blessed by this enigmatic peasant woman from India. At one point I get up to check in back of the curtain behind Ammachi but, incredibly, there is no electric motor running there. Where then is the powerful, pulsating energy I feel coming from?

At last it is my turn; I kneel hesitantly before Ammachi. The total compassionate acceptance emanating from her completely disarms me. For once in my life, I lay down my sword and my shield. I plunge into Amma's lap, throwing my arms around her waist, burying my head beneath her ribs. I am pitched into blackness. I reach out to Amma with all of my heart and find in her— nothing. There is absolutely nothing there. And yet in this vast emptiness which seems to engulf me, I sense something—conscious. It feels as if the nothingness of all of space and time is smiling. I pull back, amazed, and look up in Amritanandamayi Ma's radiant eyes. I understand that this is an untruthworthy emotional reaction, but for one moment I find myself believing that, Yes, this is for real. The teachings of the yogis are true. There is a state of luminous clarity that transcends and permeates everything. By revealing the divinity in herself, Ammachi is showing us the heart of reality: our own divine essence.

Behind me the brahmacharins sing a traditional Malalayam *bhajan* to Devi, the Supreme Goddess:

> Who knows Thy greatness,
> O Thou who art the substratum
> Of this illusory world?
> Thousands and thousands of living beings
> Seek Thy divine, radiant smile!
> Who knows Thy greatness
> O Mother, who knows?

INCARNATING
THE FEMININE DIVINE

*B*efore the beginning she existed as a mass of consciousness, limitless, self-aware, self-willed. Bored with her own unchanging perfection, she projected a cosmos out of a fraction of a fraction of her formless being. Flecks of foam in this vast ocean of conscious energy congealed into discrete universes. Some of these energies took up their places as the Gods and Goddesses of the world systems.

In the great, silent expanse, the Goddess Bhumeshvari began to praise the Universal Mother; consequently life erupted on her shores. Continents took shape, coalesced, broke apart. Beings of all shapes and intelligences worshiped on the lands and in the waters. And, in the era of Vaivasvata the progenitor, on the continent of Jambudvipa where the Sarasvati River, five miles wide, bathed the fertile Indus Valley, a race of humanity began to flourish. From paleolithic times, there as everywhere women and men took birth, the Mother was revered.

This is not a myth, but the inner history of our world. If some part of you responds, it is because the Mother herself is using your eyes to read these words, is lifting your fingers to turn these pages, is suspecting her all-pervading existence in the stirrings of your intellect. She is what you really are—a mass of consciousness, limitless, self-aware.

"How long does it take to realize the Goddess? To become one with Her?" I ask Swami Veda Bharati.

"The blink of an eye," he smiles. "All it requires is a glance from the Mother of the Universe." And then, because he loves to tell stories, Swami Veda speaks of the Gods. Brahma, the creator of our particular universe (there are, of course, many others) lives for 311,040,000,000,000 of our earth years. Everything that we experience as real is merely Brahma's dream. But Brahma himself was born from the dream of Vishnu, an infinitely vaster intelligence. A thousand times the length of Brahma's life is just a few hours to Vishnu who himself lives some 671,846,400,000,000,000,000 of our years, according to the reckoning of the yogis. Brahma is born and dies, is reborn and dies again, over and over in the boundlessness of Vishnu's dream, creating galaxies, withdrawing them, creating galaxies, withdrawing them. In every instant untold millions of other Brahmas are also taking birth and dying in Vishnu's being.

But all of Vishnu's existence is barely a breath in the lifespan of Mahadeva, "the Great God": Shiva himself. Millions and billions of Vishnus are taking birth at every moment in the infinity of Shiva's meditation. And the yoginis, who should know, say Shiva himself lives for 87,071,293,440,000,000,000,000,000,000,000,000 of our years. At the end of that eternity, even Shiva must pass away.

"And 1,000 of Shiva's lifespans," Swami Veda closes his eyes, "is one glance from the Mother of the Universe."

She is Maha Kali, the Devourer, eternity itself. But because she is beyond time she can manifest in time. Because she is limitless, she can limit herself. "The supremely auspicious One, my Mother, is ever pure and transparent. She is wider than space itself and tinier than an atom. She is omniscient, yet she knows nothing; she does everything, yet she never acts; she holds everyone, yet no one holds her. All forms exist in her, but she is formless. Everything belongs to her, but she claims nothing. Through her everything that can be known is known, and yet she cannot be known. She is bliss, yet she herself is beyond bliss. Everything, even the gods, vanish into her; she alone never dies. She has no father or mother, yet innumerable are her daughters, like me," the seeress Hemalekha taught her husband.

The matrix of being is without limit yet She measures the measureless. That is why the sages call her Maya, "the measurer." She gives us the idea that the stars can be counted, and that our own lives have a beginning and an end. This is so that we can grasp what she herself cannot: finitude.

Watching Sri Ma sit before her *linga,* reciting mantras ancient before the God of my own culture was born, and then merging into perfect stillness, I realize that the Goddess dwells beyond the outer reaches of thought, yet because she is the source of sound, those who listen to silence can hear her speak. The voice of the Goddess resounds "like thunder in the sky of the mind" according to the Tantra:

"I am the intelligence from which the universe emanates and in which it inheres, like a reflection in a mirror. The ignorant believe I am merely inert matter, but the wise experience me as the true Self within themselves. They glimpse me when their minds become as still and clear as an ocean without waves.

"Brahma, Vishnu, Shiva, the Gods of all the directions and their energies, indeed every entity on all planes of existence, are manifestations of myself. My power is too vast to be imagined. Yet beings do not know me because their minds are shrouded in ignorance. That too is my power.

"The supreme wisdom is that which ends the delusion that anyone or anything exists apart from myself. The fruit of this realization is fearlessness and the end of sorrow. When one realizes that all the limitless universes are a fraction of an atom in the unity of my being, that all the numberless lives in the universes are a wisp of vapor in one of my breaths, that all the triumphs and tragedies, the good and evil in all the worlds, are merely my unconsidered, spontaneous play, then life and death stand still, and the drama of individual life evaporates like a shallow pond on a warm day.

"You are experiencing me now, yet you do not recognize me. There is no remedy for your ignorance other than to worship me as your innermost Self. Surrender yourself to me with joyful, one-pointed devotion, and I will help you discover your true being. Abide in consciousness as continuously and effortlessly as the ignorant abide in their bodies. Abide in me as I abide in you. Know that even now there is absolutely no difference between us. Realize it now!"

"That which shines within as pure Being is her majesty, the Supreme Empress, Absolute Consciousness," concludes the *Tripura Rahasya*. "The universe and all the creatures that range within it are that One Reality; yes, all this is she alone."

When the Tantra describes the Goddess, it is not talking about a multi-armed female deity in a sari. Nor is it speaking of her the ancient Greeks called Gaia (the Hindus call her Bhumeshvari, "Goddess of the Earth") because the earth will perish and the Goddess will not. She is what remains after the cosmos itself has dissolved, after every last proton has decayed and the final wave of energy has dissipated. And from the infinite emptiness of her being new universes will again burst forth. Without end. Because she is not bothered with beginnings or endings. She is Reality. She is what is, whether anything else at all is or is not.

This Goddess—you cannot ask how she came to be, because she never came into existence; she is what we mortals call existence. You cannot say she is just a myth, because something exists, or even the dream of our lives could never have been dreamt. Whatever it is that is the root of you and me and the saints and the planets and the stars and the space between the stars—that is she. Our scientists know that she is there and that she is awesome, but they don't know how to describe her (though they struggle with their equations) and they don't realize she is conscious—though her level of consciousness is something infinitely beyond our understanding. They certainly never imagine that in her omnipotence she can assume a human body and walk among us; that in fact she has assumed the body that is holding this book!

This, at least, is the belief of the *shaktas,* the devotees of the Goddess in India. They claim theirs is the most ancient of all religions, and that is why Shaktism permeates most other schools of Indian thought and praxis: it is the very heart of Tantra. The women saints of India espouse this view, though they use different terms to express it. They differ from us in that they seek not to learn or to teach about the Goddess, but to wholly embody her. Because they incarnate the divine, unselfconsciously they evoke her in us.

Lest this sound too abstract, let me assure you that in India the Goddess's living presence is felt very concretely. The Indians have a saying. "In public, a Vaishnava." At public gatherings one joins the masses in singing the names of the popular gods with whole-hearted devotion. *Jai Rama! Hare Krishna!* "With one's inner circle, a Shaivite." Quietly, with those of more subtle understanding, one discusses the Tantra. Devoted to the philosophy of Shiva—the unitary consciousness behind all phenomena—one practices the inner disciplines of yoga. "But in one's heart, a Shakta." Whatever one's religious orientation, whether he or she is a devotee of Rama, of the more recent Semitic avatar Jesus, of Shiva, or of the formless being the Vedas call Brahman, at the core of their beings Hindus know they are children of the Divine Mother. The greatest of India's women saints know this in every breath they take, and express it in their every action. I am not being glib. One need look no further than Anandamayi Ma or Ammachi to see that this is literally true.

In Hindu theology the ultimate reality is something utterly beyond our ability to conceive, and yet—as if she actually cares about us—the Goddess breaks into history to shatter our cozy view of material existence and give us a glimpse of something wholly other, something transcendently divine, yet entirely intimate. One such encounter is metaphorically described in the *Devi Mahatmyam,* "The Glory of the Goddess," perhaps the most frequently recited scripture in India, often simply called the *Chandi.* This is the text Sri Ma performs every day at her Mandir. Let me tell you that story because it illuminates this great paradox in the Goddess's nature and leads us back to the paradox in ours.

Self Discipline, Universal Love, Selfless Service and the other divine beings have been cast out of heaven, routed by the fiercest, strongest, most thoroughly diabolical warrior they have ever encountered: Egotism. Ego disregards the promptings of Spirit and claims all he sees, living for sensual pleasure and self-glorification, aided by fawning minions like Greed, Lust, and Anger.

The divine beings run to the greatest of all the gods, Brahma, Vishnu and Shiva, to plead for help. But when the Big Three realize who they are up against, they exchange worried glances. "This job is too much for the three of us," they agree. "In a case like this, there is only one recourse." And sitting down for meditation, the gods concentrate their mental energy on her, the Supreme Goddess. Her response is instantaneous.

At that very moment as Greed and Lust are trampling the world, their attention is rivetted by an extraordinarily beautiful woman seated quietly near a mountain top. "She's incredible!" they pant. "Ego must possess her!" And indeed when Ego hears about her ravishing beauty he sends his henchmen to her with a proposal.

"Submit to Ego and all the wealth of the world will be yours!" the demons announce to this mysterious woman. "Become his slave and we will serve you forever!"

Smiling shyly, she responds, "Oh my, that's a very attractive offer. But—silly me—I took a foolish vow when I was a little girl that I would only marry the man who defeats me in battle. I'm afraid I cannot accept your master unless he conquers me."

Ego is enraged at this reply and sends his generals Fear and Revenge with their heavily armed divisions to take the mysterious beauty by force. As the demons reach out to grasp her, however, the delicate maiden begins to grow—and grow—and grow. An extra eye swells from her forehead, numerous arms sprout from her trunk, and fangs erupt from her howling mouth. Swords, spears, cudgels, whirling discuses with very sharp edges—every conceivable weapon appears in each of her numberless fists. The tawny rock on which she has been sitting unfurls into an enormous, razor-clawed, ravenous lion.

"I think we bit off more than we can chew," Fear mutters under his breath as he leads the suicide charge against Durga, the Mother of the Universe.

The enemy the Ego has unwittingly engaged is the *Chit Shakti* herself—the purifying power of Supreme Consciousness. The Ego has finally confronted the Higher Self—and it is mighty! The Divine Warrioress thwarts her foes with powerful mantras, the sword of discrimination, the bow of determination, and the bludgeon of persistent yogic practice. A fierce and grisly battle ensues in which Egotism expends every means at its disposal to overcome the spiritual force within as it reasserts its innate sovereignty.

The fighting is portrayed in detail, including Mother Durga's famous battle with *Rakta Bija* ("Red Drop"): each time a drop of his blood, spilled in battle, touches the earth, it leaps up as a new warrior. The Divine Mother transforms herself into the gruesome Goddess Kali, who swallows every drop of blood before it reaches the ground. To the casual reader this is a grotesque episode, but meditators will instantly recognize the analogy: in the struggle to control one's thoughts and desires, they seem to replicate magically and maniacally. Only by catching them before they have the opportunity to take root can this endless cycle be stopped.

In the best known episode of the *Chandi,* the all-powerful demon Mahisha (Self-Delusion) lurches into battle, transforming himself from one shape into another as he attempts to elude the Universal Mother. Indeed many of us have experienced this shapeshifting as, for example, brash egotism sublimates itself into spiritual pride. He is in the form of a half man/half water buffalo when the Divine Force finally overcomes him. Indian religious art is replete with paintings and sculptures of the calm, benign Mother Durga slaying the buffalo demon Mahisha.

At one point the Universal Mother projects millions of goddesses from herself, including Brahmani, the Goddess of Prudently Applied Intelligence, Vaishnavi, Goddess of Wisely Used Material Resources, and Varahi, the Goddess of Desire for Spiritual Perfection. Ego cries out, "This is no fair!" and the Goddess reabsorbs her emanations, leading to the climatic scene in which Ego and Pure Spiritual Awareness stride forth to battle each other—alone.

In this final confrontation the *ahankara,* or sense of limited selfhood, stands unsupported by the *chitta* or *vasanas* (memories and urges of the unconscious mind). Maha Maya withdraws her delusory projections, allowing the Ego to face directly the all-pervading reality of limitless awareness. At this point the Ego can pull back into the cocoon of contracted individuality, or offer itself completely to infinity. If Ego surrenders, it wins; self finds within itself the Self of All. But Durga, the Divine Consciousness, has invited us to engage with her in a battle only she can win. The blazing lightning of *kundalini* strikes and the self dissolves—into everything.

When the Ego perishes, order is restored to the universe and harmony returns to nature. Indra and the other Gods regain their place in heaven (i.e., the mind and senses, in service of the Divine, resume their functions). They thank the Goddess and request that whenever the need for divine help arises, she reappear. "Whenever there is oppression in the world, I shall descend and destroy it," she promises.

Western scholars have made short work of this myth: it signifies a longing to return to the womb, a regressive and pathological condition of psychological annihilation. The final confrontation with the Goddess is seen differently in India because there it is recognized that only the greatest masters have sought and found and been vanquished by her.

The Goddess slew Ramana Maharshi when he was seventeen years old. For the rest of his life the *pashus* (bound souls) experienced sublimity in his silent presence. (*Tripura Rahasya,* the Goddess text I have quoted above, was his favorite scripture.) She took Adi Shankaracharya's life when he was eight, bathing by the river outside his village. His masterpiece *Saundarya Lahari Ananda Lahari* ("Waves of Beauty, Waves of Bliss"), written twenty years later, shortly before his physical death, consists of one hundred verses in praise of this Goddess. It is considered the finest poem in the Sanskrit language. Ammachi was still a young girl when a blazing mass of golden light suffused her being and commanded her to serve all beings. Each master in his or her own way came to embody the Goddess—not to "return to the womb" but to return to the root of their own being, of the being of all.

Sri Aurobindo, the sage of Pondicherry, celebrated this union in his beautiful booklet, *The Mother,* when he wrote that the last stage of perfection occurs "when you are completely identified with the Divine Mother and feel yourself to be no longer another and separate being, instrument, servant, or worker but truly a child and eternal portion of her consciousness and force. Always she will be in you and you in her: it will be your constant, simple, and natural experience that all your thought and seeing and action, your very breathing or moving come from her and are hers." In that unending moment you are consciously "an outflow from the Supreme, a divine movement of the Eternal."

Let me clarify that when scriptures like the *Chandi* or sages like Aurobindo call ultimate reality "she," they are not at all implying that self existent being is female. This would be as absurd as the Western notion that God is male. Formless consciousness is as genderless as it is bodiless and thoughtless. Nevertheless, from ages immemorial sages have observed that that which substands the universe behaves like a mother. It manifested the worlds out of its own womblike essence. It fosters life. The forms it projects are beautiful. And when we err against its laws, it patiently corrects us. The sages look at this apparent action of actionless being and called it that most beautiful and most primal of Sanskrit words: *"Ma."*

The paradox that a consciousness vast enough to encompass all the dimensions of all the simultaneously appearing universes could intervene in our lives is played out on several levels. One is the appearance of the Goddess in any of her numerous guises in the life-transforming visions of those who call out to her—and sometimes to those who hadn't realized they were calling. Don't be misled: Kali and Lakshmi and Saravati are appearing to Hindus now in India and Mauritius and Detroit even as the Madonna appears to Catholics at Medjugoria and Quan Yin to Chinese sailors in the Yellow Sea. The Hindu would, of course, instantly recognize these apparitions as yet more revelatory disguises of the Mother.

But it is said that whenever she so wills, the Mother also assumes a human body. According to two of India's greatest spiritual classics, the *Devi Bhagavatam* and the *Markandeya Purana,* the Goddess fulfilled her vow to descend to put and end to oppression in the world at the end of the last age by incarnating as Krishna Vasudeva. Krishna is believed by many Hindus to have been an avatar and is known by Western yoga students as the illumined speaker of the *Bhagavad Gita.* Krishna's machinations helped lead to the true first world war, described in the *Mahabharata,* in which the advanced Indus/Sarasvati valley civilization which flourished from at least 6,000 B.C.E. to circa 3,000 B.C.E., was virtually annihilated. This time the demons the Goddess came to destroy were human—Prince Duryodhana and his henchmen—and the cost to humanity was the collapse of that era's leading culture.

"In the past the Divine Mother had to kill the demons," says Swami Amritsvarupananda, a *sannyasin* from South India. Referring to great contemporary women saints like Ammachi, he adds, "Today the Divine Mother kills the demons within us. Now she conquers us with love." It behooves us to respond to her love before she resorts again to methods that are more extreme. Given that our present culture is devastating the ecosphere, making the depredations of tyrants like Duryodhana look like Boy Scout camp-outs in comparison, an intervention by a fiercer form of the Mother may be imminent.

The scriptures state that the Goddess manifested all the dimensions of space and time out of "a fraction of a fraction" of her majesty. She is everything that exists, and yet is infinitely, infinitely more. Today many feminists, in their eagerness to reestablish a link with earth energy and the value of physicality, reject the transcendent aspects of the Goddess. From the Shakta point of view, this is like taking home a photograph of one's newborn and showing it to everyone, saying "Here's my new baby!" while the infant remains forgotten at the hospital.

As I read through the tantric literature I find the texts reiterating again and again that Rajarajeshvari, "the Supreme Sovereign Empress," is wholly transcendent, and yet she is completely, fully, consciously present in every atom in space. In this theology, to be transcendent means to be imminent in every fleck of matter, in every pulse of energy, in every beating heart. Therefore every object and every human action is sacred, or can be sacred when its innate divinity is respected. This understanding forms the basis of tantric ritualism. It reveres the world. It sanctifies even the "ugly" face of the world: disease, decrepitude, death. It forcefully exhorts us to fulfill our responsibilities in the world. But it never mistakes the world for the reality underlying it. Worlds come and go. The Goddess remains.

In order to understand what a Hindu sees when she looks at an enlightened woman, it is necessary to come to terms with a worldview which includes an utterly transcendent Goddess who nevertheless is moved by compassion to act in the world, and the capacity of human beings to serve as vehicles for her sublime wisdom energy. When Sri Ma steps into a street in India, people throw themselves to the ground in front of her. They are prostrating not to an Assamese village woman, but to a conscious force that exists beyond space and time. Not every rickshaw driver in Calcutta will articulate for you this theology, but each devotee pressing his head to the earth before Sri Ma feels it. They were raised with this understanding. It is the soul of India. It is, perhaps, the soul of the world.

How can one tell if one is in the presence of a true saint? The real saint understands that the devotees making obseisance before her are in fact offering homage to the cosmic matrix. In the past several decades we in the West have beheld the sad spectacle of spiritual teachers who appropriated that reverence for themselves. In India it is more difficult for articulate but egotistical speakers to set themselves up as gurus. With thousands of years of experience, Indians can tell when it is the Mother's radiance shining through a human frame, and when it is Mahisha's, that clever, shapeshifting demon of self-aggrandizement.

How can it be that we Westerners, with all our worldly wisdom, have lost the ability to distinguish a saint from a snake oil peddler? I wonder if it was when we lost the Goddess, when we started telling ourselves that we are basically sinful rather than essentially divine, when we accepted that God embodied himself on earth only once rather than that the Goddess is incarnating here continuously, in every age, in every culture, when we lost the sense that to look into the face of God we need look no further than the person sitting next to us. We gave away our spiritual authority, handing the key to heaven to an enclave of priests who seem to have misplaced it. Now we are locked out of our own divine being. And any rascal who comes along insisting he can get us back in looks good to us!

The women saints I have been privileged to meet are in a very real sense the antithesis of the religious preachers of the West. They don't tell us what to believe but show us how to live. Rather than condemning those whose mores differ from theirs, they serve them. Rather than insisting that one particular party has exclusive claim to saving knowledge while everyone else is eternally condemned, they quietly suggest that a divine light shines in every heart; we have only to remove the bushel basket covering the flame. Today's televangelists look suspiciously like Mahishas to me, but my vision is biased now, having sat with teachers who did not let ego or doctrine come between them and their fellow souls.

To be egoless is not to be colorless; in fact the woman saints I've met are prisms though which many hues of the divine refract. They have distinctive personalities and great personal strength. But their personality is not what is "real" about them: their spiritual life is the *shakti* emanating from them, the Goddess's energy.

As a contemporary Western woman my encounters with Indian saints have not been entirely rhapsodic. We women of the West have just begun to reject humility and selflessness as the shackles of a patriarchal society, when these woman appear to tell us these are not anti-feminine values, but genuine spiritual ones. We have just begun to develop egos and these women direct us toward egolessness. We are just beginning to get comfortable with our bodies when they tell us our bodies are the least that we are. More than once my response to these women has not been melting surrender but sputtering feminism.

Like adolescents, we have been struggling to break free from our own mothers and from their ideas about what we as women can and should be. India's saints point us not toward what we desire to be but what we truly are, beyond any identification with our mother, our clan, our species, our planet. They direct us to the soul of nature, the heart of spirit: to our innermost truth. There we will find *ananda*, bliss, they claim. And then we, like them, must share it.

Perhaps it will help to point out that when Indian women of spirit teach humility and selflessness, they are speaking to men as well as to women. Furthermore, their lives reveal that true humility is rooted in unshakable strength, and selflessness in a profound understanding of the workings of self. They have become not merely servants of humanity but *devis*, goddesses, transparent to the brilliance of divinity yet adamantine as diamond. If you don't believe me, go sit in their presence. If you cannot find the Goddess in yourself, you will surely see her in them. Look into Sri Ma's face, or Gurumayi's. It is a mirror. See your Self there.

What does an enlightened woman see when she looks at us? A mass of consciousness, limitless, self aware. She sees herself. "When the sage sees the Self in all beings, and all beings in the Self, that seer loves everyone, everything," says the Veda.

May we all abide in that love.

For centuries the wisdom of India's women of spirit was South Asia's best kept secret. Today Nirmala Devi initiates the British in *sahaja yoga* while Meera Ma bathes all Germany in the radiance of her enlightened presence from Thalheim. Ammachi introduces Stockholm to the purest essence of Tantra while Gurumayi opens a new meditation center near Melbourne.

Today in the West we talk of the Goddess returning. If India's "divine mothers" are any indication, she is bringing her daughters with her, and in full force. Like a purifying tide, the sanctity of these women, once reserved for their families, is beginning to envelop the world.

Resources

For more information about the women profiled in this book, please contact the following organizations. If you have stories of your own to share about your experiences with women of spirit, please feel free to contact Linda Johnsen c/o Yes International Publishers.

Sri Ma: Devi Mandir, 5950 Highway 128, Napa, CA 94558. The Devi Mandir (Sanskrit for "Goddess Temple") is also the best U.S. resource for information about traditional yogic methods of worshiping the Divine Mother.

Anandamayi Ma: Matri Satsang, P.O. Box 876, Encinitas, CA 92024. I strongly recommend "Sri Anandamayi Ma: Her Life, Her Message," an extraordinary videotape available through Matri Satsang which includes rare film footage of "the bliss permeated mother" from the last few years of her life.

Anandi Ma: Dhyanyoga Center, P.O.Box 3194, Antioch, CA 94531. Anandi Ma also has centers in Woodbury, CT and Portland, ME. She spends much of the year in the U.S. and is very accessible.

Gurumayi: SYDA Foundation, P.O. Box 600, South Fallsburg, NY 12779. The videotapes, audiocassettes and CDs produced by SYDA are pricey but unsurpassed in quality. SYDA's monthly magazine *Darshan* is one of the finest spiritual periodicals in the world.

Ma Yoga Shakti: Ma Yoga Shakti International Mission, 114-23 Lefferts Blvd., South Ozone Park, NY 11420. Ma Yoga Shakti is the author of several authoritative books and pamphlets on yogic techniques and spiritual philosophy.

Ammachi: M.A. Center, P.O. Box 613, San Ramon, CA 94583. Swami Amritsvarupananda's compilation of Ammachi's informal talks with visitors and disciples *(Awaken Children! Conversations with Mata Amritanandamayi,* multiple volumes, M.A. Center, San Ramon, CA) is the most comprehensive and inspiring account of a saint's day to day life since Mohendranath Gupta's *Gospel of Sri Ramakrishna.*

Further Reading

As the Flower Sheds Its Fragrance, Atmananda. Shree Shree Anandamayee Charitable Society: Calcutta, 1983. Vivid personal account of Anandamayi Ma compiled by Ma's English translator.

Ashes at my Guru's Feet, Gurumayi Chidvilasananda. SYDA Foundation: South Fallsburg, NY, 1990. An amazingly intimate poetic description of Gurumayi's spiritual journey.

The Concise Yoga Vasistha, Swami Venkatesananda. State University of New York Press: Albany, NY, 1984. The astonishing (and voluminous!) *Yoga Vasistha* is well worth reading in its entirety, but if time does not permit you to read the third longest book in world literature, this abridgement summarizes the stories of mythical yoginis like Lila, devotee of the goddess Sarasvati, and Chudala, queen of Malava.

Gauri Mata, Saradeswari Asram. Saradeswari Asram: Calcutta, n.d. Biography of Gauri Ma, founder of the Free School for Hindu Girls. Gauri Ma (1858-1938) renounced a life of luxury to devote herself to spiritual practice, and later renounced solitary discipline for social service.

Great Women of India, Swami Madhavananda and Ramesh Chandra Majumdar, eds. Advaita Ashrama: Mayavati, India, 1953. A comprehensive survey of remarkable women in India's history and mythology, many of whom were spiritual giants.

Hidden Journey, Andrew Harvey. Harvey's poetic account of his encounter with Meera Ma, a radiant embodiment of the Divine Mother presently living near Frankfurt, Germany.

Holy Mother, Swami Nikhilananda. Ramakrishna-Vivekananda Center: New York, 1982. Biography of Sarada Devi, a Bengali village girl revered as an incarnation of the Divine Mother.

Kindle My Heart: Wisdom and Inspiration from a Living Master, Vol. I, Gurumayi Chidvilasananda. Prentice Hall: NY, 1989. Talks by Gurumayi. Vol. II published by Simon & Schuster: NY, 1992.

Lalleshwari: Spiritual Poems by a Great Siddha Yogini, Swami Muktananda. Gurudev Siddha Peeth: Ganeshpuri (India), 1981. A short but very readable retelling of the life and teachings of the 14th century Kashmiri Shaivite master Lalla.

Mata Amritanandamayi, Amritatma Chaitanya. Mata Amritanandamayi Mission Trust: Vallickavu (India), 1988. Biography of Ammachi, who despite a childhood of physical and psychological abuse, matured into one of the greatest saints in India today.

Matri Darshan: A Photo Album About Shri Anandamayi Ma, Atmananda, et al., trs. Mangalam Verlag S. Schang: Allemagne (Germany), 1988. Exquisite photographs of Anandamayi Ma, with quotations from her teachings in English, German and French.

Mother of All, Richard Schiffman. Sree Viswa Jananee Parishat: Jillellamudi (India), 1983. The life of Anasuya Devi (Jillellamudi Ma), who demonstrated that a woman can be a housewife and the Mother of the World at the same time!

One Life's Pilgrimage, Srimata Gayatri Devi. Vedanta Center: Co-hasset, MA, 1977. Biography the first sannyasini to teach in America. Gayatri Devi, quite elderly now, remains the spiritual director of the Ananda Ashram founded by Swami Paramananda in La Crescenta, California.

Sweetness and Light: Life and Teachings of Godavari Mataji, Mani Sahukar. Bharatiya Vidya Bhavan: Bombay, 1966. Life story of Godavari Ma, successor to Upansani Baba, the controversial yogi who shocked India by preaching the spiritual superiority of women.

They Lived with God: Life Stories of Some Devotees of Sri Ramakrishna, Swami Chetananda. Vedanta Society of St. Louis: St. Louis, 1989. Includes accounts of the lives of the 19th century Bengali mystic's major women disciples, some of whom went on to become saints in their own right.

Tripura Rahasya (or *The Mystery beyond the Trinity),* Ramanananda Saraswathi, trs. T.N. Venkataraman: Tiruvannamalai (India), 1980. This is probably the greatest classic produced by the Shaktas (Hindu devotees of the Divine Mother) since the midieval period. In addition to describing who and what the Goddess really is, and how to experience Her (and what will happen to you when you do!), it narrates the life story and mind shattering teachings of the yogini Hemalekha.

Women Saints East and West, Swami Ghanananda and John Stewart-Wallace, eds. Vedanta Press, Hollywood, 1955. A classic compendium of spiritual biographies.

Glossary

adhikara	Qualifications which must be met before one is considered fit to receive sacred knowledge.
adi shakti	Primordial consciousness/energy.
ahankara	Sense of oneself as an individual being.
ahimsa	Nonviolence. Never harming others is the first rule of yoga practice.
akka	Elder sister.
ananda	Bliss.
arati	Ritual in which a deity or guru is honored with mantras and the waving of lights.
avadhuta	Saint whose center of awareness is established beyond mind. Often perceived by others as crazy or amoral.
avatar	An incarnation of divinity.
Ayurveda	The ancient system of medicine native to India.
bedi	A mound of earth or concrete surrounding a sacred tree.
bhajan	Devotional song.
Bhagavad Gita	Literally "the song of God." Consists of an especially sacred portion of the Indian epic *Mahabharata* in which Krishna (see below) encourages the warrior prince Arjuna to go to battle against a tyrant. In the course of the conversation Krishna also reveals the nature of reality!
bhairavi	Tantric yogini.
bhakti	Devotion to the divine.
bhang	Hashish.
Bhumeshvari	Earth goddess.
bhumi	The earth.
Brahma	The god who created this universe. (In Hindu cosomology, many other universes also exist.)
Brahman	Ultimate reality, characterized by being, consciousness and bliss.
brahmacharin	Literally "one who walks in God." Celibate student committed to spiritual life.
brahmarishi	Literally "God seer." Honorific for a select group of specially revered Vedic sages.
brahmin	Member of India's priestly caste.
chakra	Vortex of consciousness/energy within the body.
chit	Consciousness.
chitta	Mind.
darshan	Literally "sight." Seeing a saint or a deity.
deva	Literally "bright being." A god.
devi	Goddess.
dharma	Religion or right action.
dhyana	Meditation.
Durga	The Divine Mother as warrior goddess, protecting Her devotees and also slaying everything in them that is less than divine.
ghee	Clarified butter. Offered to the sacred fire during Hindu rituals. Also used to auspicious effect in Indian cooking!

gopi	Milkmaids of Vrindavan who fell in love with the cowherd/prince Krishna.
griham	Home or house.
grihasthashrami	Literally "one who makes his home his ashram." Householder.
jagad guru	World teacher.
japa	Mantra repetition.
jnana	Divine knowledge.
Kali	Fierce form of the Goddess.
kanchukas	Contractions of all pervading consciousness which make finite awareness possible.
kanya kumari puja	Rite in which a young girl is worshiped as the Goddess.
kanyadin	Hindu convent.
karma	Action and its consequences.
kheyal	Inner guide.
kirtan	Devotional singing.
Krishna	Prince of Mathura who lived about 3000 B.C.E. He is believed by many Indians to have been an avatar and is the focus of tremendous religious devotion.
kriya	Involuntary movements during which blocks to the flow of kundalini are snapped loose.
kumbha mela	Religious festival held at the confluence of the Yamuna and Ganges rivers every four years. As many as 30 million pilgrims gather for this event, making it the largest ritual convocation in the world.
kundalini	The energy of consciousness as it manifests in a physical body.
Lakshmi	Goddess of prosperity and good fortune.
linga	Sacred stone emblematic of Shiva.
Ma	Literally "Mother." Women saints and also the Goddess herself are frequently referred to as Ma in India.
maha	Literally "great" as in mahatma, "great soul" or mahadeva, "great god," mahavidya or "great science."
mandala	Yantra in which a deity has been installed.
mandir	Temple.
mantra	Sacred words or sounds. Meditating on a mantra (considered the "vibratory body" of a deity) is said to lead one to higher states of consciousness.
maya	Term used in the Vedas to signify "the glory of the Goddess," i.e., material manifestation. Later came to suggest the illusory (i.e., transient and sublatable) nature of the universe.
moksha	Spiritual liberation.
nada	Divine sound.
namaha	Literally "I offer my respect to."
nirvikalpa samadhi	Deep state of meditation in which unity of the meditator, object of meditation and process of meditation is experienced. Experiential realization of nonduality.
paramahansa	Literally "great swan." Honorific for a God realized soul.
Parashakti	Literally "the Supreme Consciousness/Energy."
Parvati	Literally "daughter of the mountain." Benign, dark complexioned goddess whose consort is Shiva, and whose sons

	are the elephant headed deity Ganesha (remover of obstacles) and Skanda (warrior god).
pashu	Literally "domestic cattle." Metaphorically a bound soul tethered to the world by his or her desires.
prana	Life force.
prasad	Food that has been offered to a deity or one's guru before being consumed. As the "left overs" from the deity's meal, it is especially auspicious.
puja	Religious ritual.
raja yoga	Classical yoga involving ethical living, physical exercises and meditation.
rajas	The force of activity.
Rama	Divine incarnation, husband of Sita, and hero of the epic *Ramayana*. Also another name for divine consciousness.
rishi	Enlightened seer.
sadashiva	Literally "true auspiciousness" or "the greatest good." The supreme reality.
sadhana	Spiritual practice.
sadhu	Renunciate who is devoting his or her life to self realization. Usually a wanderer.
sahaja samadhi	Literally "natural meditation." The state of one whose mind never leaves the divine.
sahasrara	Literally "one thousand petals." The chakra corresponding to the cerebral cortex.
sakshin	Inner witness. Higher Self.
samadhi	Deepest state of meditation.
samskara	Unconscious tendency. May be brought over from a soul's previous birth.
sanatana	Eternal.
sannyas	Formal renunciation.
sannyasini	Hindu nun.
Sarasvati	Goddess of wisdom and the arts.
sat	Being. Truth.
satsang	Literally "keeping the company of truth." Spiritual fellowship.
sattva	The force of harmony.
satguru	Literally "true spiritual teacher." One's spiritual master.
satya	Truthfulness.
seva	Selfless service.
Shaivism	School of Indian thought and praxis devoted to Shiva.
shakta	A devotee of Shakti.
Shakti	Spiritual energy. The supreme consciousness force: the Goddess.
shaktipat	The transmission of the enlightenment energy of a guru lineage.
Shaktism	Goddess tradition of India.
shastra	Scripture.
Shiva	God of destruction/transformation. Also a masculine name for the divine consciousness, in contradistinction to Shakti.
siddha	Literally "the perfected one." An enlightened master.
siddhasana	Literally "perfect seat." A yogic meditation posture.
siddhi	Occult power.

sri	Woman's title of great respect. Pronounced "shree."
Sri Vidya	Literally "the supreme science." Major school of Shaktism. Also a name of the Goddess.
sundari	Beauty.
svarga	Heaven.
tamas	The force of inertia.
tapas, tapasya	Spiritual self discipline.
tattva	Element or principle.
tejas	Spiritual lustre.
Tripura Sundari	Literally "the Greatest Beauty in the Three Worlds." The Supreme Goddess.
turiya	Literally "the fourth." The state of consciousness beyond waking, dream and sleep states.
Vaishnava	Devotee of the god Vishnu or his avatars Rama or Krishna.
vasana	Mental tendency. A "groove" in the recording equipment of the mind.
Veda	Ancient (7000 - 1500 B.C.E.) scripture of India.
vira	Heroic.
Vishnu	God who presides over the maintenance of the universe.
viveka	Discrimination between the eternal and the ephemeral.
yantra	Geometric design used as a focus for yogic concentration.
yogi	Male yogini.
yogini	Woman who uses the techniques of yoga to seat herself in her divine nature.